Meeting Challenges

UNSHAKEN BY LIFE'S
UPS AND DOWNS

Ringu Tulku Rinpoche

Edited by David Cowey, Maeve O'Sullivan
and Mary Heneghan

Bodhicharya
PUBLICATIONS
Awaken the heart by opening the mind

First published in 2018 by
BODHICHARYA PUBLICATIONS
Bodhicharya Publications is a Community Interest Company registered in the UK.
38 Moreland Avenue, Hereford, HR1 1BN, UK
www.bodhicharya.org Email: publications@bodhicharya.org

ISBN 978-0-9957343-2-6
First edition: December 2018

Compiled and edited by David Cowey and Mary Heneghan, with help from Maeve O'Sullivan.

Teaching sources:

Main teaching source: *'Transforming Suffering and Happiness'* by the Third Do Drupchen Rinpoche, Jigme Tenpa Nyima. Given by Ringu Tulku Rinpoche at Bodhicharya Berlin, Germany. August 2010.

Transcribed by Birgit Khoury, Tara Woolnough and David Cowey. First edit by David Cowey.

Subsidiary teaching source: *'Carrying the Wind:' Instructions on 'Shidug Lamkhyer' - How to Bring Joy & Sorrow onto the Path* - written by the Third Do Drubchen. Given by Ringu Tulku Rinpoche at Karma Chang Chub Chö Phel Ling in Heidelberg, Germany. October 1998.

Transcribed and first edit by Gabriele Hollmann.

Further editing by Mary Heneghan, with editorial comments and input from Maeve O'Sullivan.

Root text translation: based on that of Adam Pearcey, 2006. www.lotsawahouse.org

Bodhicharya Publications team for this book: David Cowey ; Mary Heneghan; Rachel Moffitt; Paul O'Connor; Maeve O'Sullivan; David Tuffield; Mariette van Lieshout.

Typesetting & Design by Paul O'Connor at judodesign.com
Cover image: Annapurna Range, Nepal, by Skouatroulio.
Printed on recycled paper by Imprint Digital, Devon, UK.

THE HEART WISDOM SERIES
By Ringu Tulku Rinpoche

The Ngöndro
Foundation Practices of Mahamudra

From Milk to Yoghurt
A Recipe for Living and Dying

Like Dreams and Clouds
Emptiness and Interdependence, Mahamudra and Dzogchen

Dealing with Emotions
Scattering the Clouds

Journey from Head to Heart
Along a Buddhist Path

Riding Stormy Waves
Victory over the Maras

Being Pure
The practice of Vajrasattva

Radiance of the Heart
Kindness, Compassion, Bodhicitta

Meeting Challenges
Unshaken by Life's Ups and Downs

'Happiness is like a lid.
Unhappiness is like cutting the edge of continuation.
Loneliness is like your companion.
Sickness is like your nurse.
Whatever state you are in,
Always cultivate this understanding.'

Traditional Kadampa saying
From Eastern Tibet

Contents

Afterword

Editor's Preface

This book is Ringu Tulku's commentary on a text called *"Bringing happiness and unhappiness onto the path"* or "Transforming suffering and happiness." The original text was written by the Third Do Drupchen Rinpoche, Jigme Tenpe Nyima, in the 19th Century.

Ringu Tulku has taught on this text many times over the years and the main body of this book was taken from a teaching he gave at Bodhicharya Berlin, in August 2010. We have added, in the creation of this book, a handful of short sections from a teaching Ringu Tulku gave in Heidelberg in 1998, on this same text.

The teaching describes how we can come to meet all our experience, both of suffering and of joy, equally; in such a way that we are not phased by either. We can bring all experience onto our path in this way, transforming it so that it does not cause ourselves, or others, problems. We don't need to be constantly rocked up and down in life by whether things are going well or not. We can find a way to be stable and at peace, regardless. This is the essential core teaching found within this book.

The original text is divided into sections looking at how we can meet suffering, and how we can meet joy, as a practice, so we remain unshaken by either. Each is dealt with from a relative perspective – that of how things commonly appear to us - and also from a more ultimate perspective - that of how things really exist. So, there are approaches given that we can start using from this very moment, as well as an over-arching view that we can work with all our life.

Some years ago, in 2007, a group of Ringu Tulku's students formed an online *Bodhicharya Study Group*, under the inspiration of Margaret Ford.

This was one of the texts we studied. As we went through it, Margaret offered questions to keep us thinking, to contemplate and discuss. I mention a couple here, in case any readers are interested to also take this approach.

At one point, Ringu Tulku discusses at some length the topic of karma. Some of the questions we contemplated were, "What was your understanding of karma before reading the text?" And, "Did that change once you had read it, and how?" Ringu Tulku talks about karma being action ~ action and reaction, cause and effect ~ which also means the term points the way towards the possibility of change and transformation. So we went on to the question, "Can you remember any times in your life where you changed your karma?"

When Ringu Tulku gets to the section about taking joy onto the path, he talks about how we can relax with what is. He explains how, if we truly understand how things are, that itself makes us gradually courageous – because we have nothing to lose. One of our questions was, "Can you think of a time in your life when you realised there was actually nothing to lose, and found courage and relaxation in that?"

It is often the case that, while working on one of Rinpoche's books such as this one, I find myself having to grapple intimately with its topic, one way or another, in my own life. I rarely escape this, and this book turned out to be no exception. While life threw up an unexpected challenge for me to meet, just as we were trying to publish this text, there was one phrase from this teaching that kept coming up in my mind:

dropping our unwillingness to suffer

It kept arising in my mind, as a kind of mantra, whenever I found myself caught up in the situation. I basically just wanted to rail against what was happening, to complain about it all and reject it. But then this line....*dropping our unwillingness to suffer*... And I would find there was a way to embrace the situation after all. It probably helped me tackle it much better than I might have otherwise. There is actually a way the challenges of life are just as okay as the rest of life. It was like:

'Here I am, a person sitting on my cushion, my breath is moving, the candle is flickering, autumn leaves are blowing outside. And I have this difficult problem in my life, which I don't know exactly how to approach yet; I don't know how, or if, it will work out yet. (In truth, it was a really upsetting problem to me.) But there can still be peace. And, amazingly, joy. Because I have, for a moment, dropped my unwillingness to suffer.'

This is something within the reach of us all (if I can manage it, even for a moment, any one of us can too). It is one thing to be peaceful in an environment where everything is taken care of for us, a protected retreat environment for example. We need those places to train ourselves, but the real practice comes amid the ups and downs of life. If we can take the next step with our practice and find a way to be peaceful even then, to meet our challenges unshaken, then we are really doing something profound and transformative for our lives. This is what Rinpoche is teaching us in this book; it is the real practice.

At the end of Rinpoche's teaching in Heidelberg, one of the organisers, while thanking him for the teachings, also turned to the audience and thanked everyone present for being interested in the teachings of the Dharma. In the words they used then, we would like to echo their appreciation and their aspiration: "We hope you will be inspired by these teachings and receive many beneficial insights from Ringu Tulku's words here, to carry with you through your life."

We offer this book with the heart wish that it may contribute to bringing ever-increasing meaning to life. May you, the reader, become unshaken by life's ups and downs. May you be unwavering on your path. Ultimately, may all beings find inner freedom, happiness and peace; through learning to dwell in equanimity, beyond all fleeting joy and sorrow.

Mary Dechen Jinpa
For Bodhicharya Publications
Holy Isle, Scotland, June 2015 & Oxford, UK, November 2018

Author of the Root Text

The teaching we are going to look at is called *Shidug Lamkhyer* in Tibetan, which literally means 'Bringing Happiness and Unhappiness onto the Path.' The author of this teaching was the Third Do Drupchen Rinpoche, Jigme Tenpe Nyima, who was a great master of the 19th Century. He had a curious name because *Do* means 'stone' and *Drubchen* means '*siddhi*' [power, attainment or accomplishment], so the name literally means 'highly attained stone.' But actually the reason he had this name was because he came from a place called Doyül - and not because he was a stone!

The First Do Drubchen lived in the later part of the 18th Century. He was one of three important students of Jigme Lingpa, who founded the *Longchen Nyingthik*, the main Nyingma teachings on Dzogchen. Another of these three students was Jigme Gyalwa Nyugu, who was the main teacher of Patrul Rinpoche (as well as Patrul Rinpoche also being a direct student of Do Drupchen Rinpoche). The Second Do Drubchen lived in the early part of the 19th Century. This text was written by the Third Do Drubchen. And now we have the Fourth Do Drubchen Rinpoche, who is also a great master, and is currently living in Sikkim, at the age of about 84 years [in 2010].

Even among great masters, the Third Do Drupchen, Jigme Tenpe Nyima, is very highly regarded. The present Dalai Lama, for example, often quotes him and remarks that, of all the Tibetan masters, he finds the writings of Do Drubchen most logical: he says that the deepest teachings and most profound philosophies are put forward particularly clearly and comprehensibly in his texts. Do Drubchen is known for that, especially regarding the most profound tantras.

So, we will go through a translation I have here of the original text, which was compiled by Adam Pearcey, [presented in *grey italics* in this volume] and discuss it as we go.

Introduction & Homage

Homage,
I pay homage to you, Noble Avalokiteshvara, recalling your qualities:
Forever joyful at the happiness of others,
And plunged into sorrow whenever they suffer.
You have fully realised Great Compassion with all its qualities,
And abide without a care for your own happiness or suffering.

Avalokiteshvara, or Chenrezig, is regarded as the Bodhisattva of compassion: the embodiment or essence of compassion. Any teaching that is concerned with Bodhisattva activity, or compassion or things like that, generally commences with a homage to Avalokiteshvara. As the homage says, he is very joyful about the happiness of others, but whenever he sees the suffering of others, he himself suffers and feels sorrow. However, because he does not care about his own happiness or suffering, in that way he is always happy. So, it is Avalokiteshvara to whom homage is paid at the start of this text. He represents the ideal of how to transform suffering and happiness.

This is an instruction indicating how to use both happiness and suffering as the path to enlightenment. This is indispensable for leading a spiritual life, a most needed tool of the Noble Ones, and quite the most priceless teaching in the world.

The teaching in this text consists of two parts: How to take unhappiness onto the path and how to take happiness onto the path.

I don't know whether we should really define these states as 'happiness' and 'unhappiness,' however. What we mean to say here is that none of us – none of all the living beings, and not only just the human beings – likes suffering. Nobody wants to have problems and pain. That is a common ground we all share and is a universal fact. Everybody wants to get rid of sufferings, pain and problems. Therefore all the beings, from the smallest, most insignificant beings to the most advanced, each and every one of us, is always engaged in the process of trying to get rid of suffering, problems and pain.

Furthermore, there is nobody who does not want to experience happiness. Any activities someone engages in, he or she is in one way or another trying to do just that, trying to get rid of suffering, trying to solve problems, trying to find a way to more happiness, more comfort and more satisfactory circumstances. The question is, however: Are we succeeding? And to what degree is it possible to succeed?

We have the continuous habit of thinking that to be free from suffering and to have happiness, we need the right things; we need the right circumstances. We think, "If all the right situations are there, then I will be happy. If I have lots of money, if I have lots of friends, if I have lots of power, then I will be happy and if not, then I will not be happy." So then we try to get those things. Sometimes we get some of them, but when we get them we often find that we are still not very happy. And in the process of getting them, we encounter all sorts of troubles and difficulties.

The idea presented here is that, instead of going through all the difficulties and making such a lot of effort to create those circumstances which might make us happy, or not unhappy, let us go directly to the actual feeling of happiness and unhappiness and try to transcend that. This is to search for a way to work directly on the experience of feeling happiness and unhappiness, rather than working at the secondary level, of what might cause us to feel happy or unhappy.

For example, I may think, "I am so unhappy because that tree outside my window does not look so nice and I have to look at it all the time. As long as that tree is there, I can't be happy." So I make myself feel that the tree is the problem, it is the cause of my unhappiness. So I fell the tree, and then I become able to see a house that was behind it. "This house, if it is there, as long as this house is there I don't have a nice view, and as long as this house, which is so tall, is there, I can't be happy." Then, if somehow this house disappears, maybe there is another house, maybe there is a mountain, or maybe there are too many cars.

If we follow our usual way of thinking, that we are unhappy because of this or because of that, there can't be any end. Then we can never ever be happy, because there is always something that is not quite right.

Therefore, if we are going to succeed in this search, we have to find another way. Another way is to work on our own feelings, so we don't keep thinking, "This is here, therefore I am unhappy." Instead, we find a way to change, to transcend, whatever feelings of dissatisfaction and unhappiness we may experience. We have to find a way to change that way of feeling directly: that is the only way; there is no other way.

But we can't only transform unhappiness in this way. We have to also transform happiness, because they are related. We might say, "I don't want unhappiness, I want happiness." But to say, "I want happiness, I want happiness", is what? Unhappiness. Although we all say that we want happiness and happiness is something very nice, this is very tricky. Wanting happiness too much becomes unhappiness.

Therefore we also need to know how to transform that longing for happiness. We can only really be happy if we can do this as well. If I can be at ease when things are not so nice, and if I can be at ease when things are very nice, then I am at ease all the time.

If we can find a way to have that result, to really learn how to do that for ourselves - to be at ease all the time without having to depend on things, situations, other people - then we have really found our inner happiness, our lasting peace. This is something really important, which is why it is described as priceless. It is something that all great beings have attained, it is their tool of liberation and happiness.

This is why I would like to try and explain this approach here, to teach how to do this. Since it is not possible to teach everything fully in a finite time, the root text states here that the author will give a partial instruction, an indication pointing out how to do this. We will then need to pick up from there and work on it ourselves.

The two parts of the teaching are:

How to use suffering as the path
How to use happiness as the path

Taking Suffering as the Path

If we begin by looking at suffering, we can first look at what our present attitude is. When we experience a little bit of suffering, or some small problem, we usually say, "That suffering is very bad; there is suffering, that is impossible; it is so bad, I cannot tolerate it, I am very unhappy."

In other words, when we experience something that is painful for our mind or body, or something that we think should not happen to us, we think, "This is not right, this is impossible; this is very bad, I don't want it; I want to get out of this immediately and never have it again."

If we are able to get out of whatever it is and never have it again, then that is fine. But that is the problem. We cannot get rid of all the causes of pain and problems. We cannot get rid of all the people who don't like us. We cannot get everybody to do whatever we want. We cannot banish everything around us, or in the world, that is not nice. That is an impossible task. The only thing that we can do is to change our attitude to this situation, in such a way that it is no longer so much of a problem for us.

One way, and maybe it is the only way, is to turn that problem into the path. What do we mean by "turn it into the path?" We mean to work on that problem, to look at it, to take it as a challenge and to use it in such a way that that problem itself becomes the solution. That is what is meant by 'transforming suffering and happiness into the path' or 'carrying suffering and happiness onto the path'.

What is a path? A path is a way forward. Working on an obstacle is the path because it gives us a way forward. If there is no obstacle there is no path, because there is nothing that you need to work on. If there is nothing you need to work on, and nothing that you need to change, then, there is no path and no need of any path. Every path means there is a problem and then we have to work on that problem, to transform it, to change it. That is a path. Using a problem and working on it, making it into 'not a problem,' is the path.

So now we can see that we need to use the problem, our unhappiness, as the path.

How to use suffering as the path to enlightenment is in two parts.

Firstly, through the truth relating to appearances:

I - Relating to How Things Appear

Whenever we are harmed by sentient beings or by anything else, if we make a habit out of perceiving only the suffering, then when even the smallest problem comes up, it will cause enormous anguish in our mind. This is because the nature of any perception or idea, whether happiness or sorrow, is to grow stronger and stronger the more we become accustomed to it.

This is what usually happens, as has already been described. When some problem arises, we say, "This is really bad!" We look at it, we think about it repeatedly, we really hold on to it. The more we say, "This is bad," the more it bothers us. And after some time it becomes impossible to deal with it. It is the same for good things as it is for bad things. If we say, "This is bad, this is really bad, this is very bad, bad, bad," then sometimes it becomes so bad that we cannot bear it at all. But similarly: "This is nice, it is really good, it is very beautiful, wonderful." Also the same! It becomes more and more beautiful, because it grows in your mind, fed and exaggerated by such thoughts. So that sometimes, maybe often, people can really make a big problem out of no problem at all.

Once I went to visit a lady I know who lived in a house with a nice view. Yet when I arrived, she was building a kind of small mountain in front of her house, so that she would no longer be able to see the view. When I asked her why she was doing this, she replied, "You see the house opposite? There is a person living there who has put their television by the window, so that I can see it and it is disturbing me." It was quite distant from her house.

So I said, "Could you not have put up a curtain?" She was adamant that she couldn't put up a curtain – but she was happy to build a small mountain instead. People do the craziest things. Because, after doing that, was the problem finished? No. If you make something into too much of a problem, if you hold onto it too much, saying, "This is so bad, it is not good," it only grows bigger.

We have to be very careful not to become too sensitive, emotionally. Otherwise, everything becomes a problem. If somebody is looking at me, "This person is looking at me. Why is this person looking at me so much?" If that person is not looking at me, "Why is this person never looking at me?" We can build up a way of being which makes everything a problem, and then even small problems can become big problems.

We also have an especially strong habitual tendency to hold onto and never let go of a problem. For example, we might have any problem, such as our watch not working, or our computer not working, or our e-mail not working. Then we tend to think, "My e-mail is not working, why is my e-mail not working? How can I be happy, if my e-mail is not working? I can never be happy, unless my e-mail is working. And if my email is working, then I can relax, only then can I really relax."

Okay, after some time, maybe I go here, I go there, I spend money, I ask people, and maybe somehow my e-mail works again. But then, my computer doesn't work. "Ah, my computer doesn't work! What to do!" Day and night: "My computer doesn't work!" I am unhappy until the computer works. And then the computer works, but something else goes wrong, or I receive a bad e-mail, an angry e-mail. Maybe not one, but two...!

Now, if we live like that, when are we going to be happy? Something is going to be not right all the time. And we cannot relax, we cannot be happy; we cannot be at ease unless there is no problem. But getting rid of all the problems is not possible, so therefore what can we do? There is only one way to deal with this kind of habit, or way of being, where we expect ourselves to be free of any problems, that everything goes well and that everything happens as we wish it.

The less we expect that everything should go well, that everything should be okay before we are okay, the more okay we actually *are*. If my e-mail doesn't work we can have the attitude, "Oh, my e-mail doesn't work, it is very nice, I don't need to write e-mails today."

If I can say that, if I can really feel, "I have a holiday today, no e-mails, this is so nice", then not having e-mail doesn't become a source of problems. Not having the e-mail is not the problem. The problem is in how I take it. Therefore if I can take what is happening in such a way that I transform it into 'not being a problem', then it is not a problem anymore.

If I take it as a problem, it is a problem; it becomes a problem. And that goes for everything. However, if my computer breaks, I could also say, "Oh, my computer is broken now. Now nobody can blame me for not writing. So I can have a nice time." This is just a small example.

Sometimes it is possible to see the even the most difficult time as something acceptable. Even pain, even death. I know people who have done that. When they were dying, they were saying, "I am so happy that now I can die so nicely. I have my teacher here now, so it is a nice time to die. It's so good, that I can die in this way, when everything is here." The process of dying is the worst, the most difficult part of life, but if someone has the capacity to find such a way of looking at it that it is not a problem, then it does not become a problem. That is what constitutes making suffering a path.

Sometimes people come to me and say, "Oh, what can I do, I have lost my partner - my girlfriend left, my boyfriend left. What can I do?" I say, "That is good, very good. You don't need these useless fellows. Now you are alone, you are free; you can do whatever you like. It could be nice, take that opportunity: you can do a retreat if you want, you can study, you can travel. Use that opportunity! And then maybe you will meet another man or woman later." This is what to do. Take it as an opportunity, and make the best use of it.

Most of us, what do we do? When we have something, we want the opposite. When we have companions, we are always fighting. When there is nobody: "Oh, I am so lonely." Since we are always looking at the negative side, at the problem side, we are never happy. We tend to treat everything around us as an enemy, as the root text says, because of our way of perceiving, because of our attitude. So it is very, very important to change that attitude. We need to change it. There is no other way; the only way to our happiness is to change our attitude.

If the way is to change our attitude, of course we should start to change in small ways. Even with very big problems, there is always a better way to see them. Even if we have an illness, or if we are dying, with much suffering and lots of problems, even then, we can always find a way to look at it in such a way that it doesn't become an overwhelming problem.

To consider sickness, for example: of course as long as we have this body, which is so delicately balanced, it is not possible to avoid sickness. One day we will get sick; one day we will die. Sooner or later everybody dies. Then, why not think, "I am sick, I am sick for sometime, but it's okay." It is better to be sick nicely, happily, than otherwise. Being unhappy that we are sick, doesn't make the sickness go away; it makes it worse.

I have been travelling to Europe and America for the last twenty years, travelling continuously in a really hectic way. When even professional travellers look at my schedule they are a little shocked and ask, "How do you manage? How many years can you do this?" And for these past twenty years I never got sick, not even for one day. I never even had a headache. I never had to cancel one talk in the last twenty years.

Now I have got a bit ill. And I have been thinking like this: "I am not really that sick, just a little bit. It is really high time for me to get a little sickness." It's very good to get sick sometimes, especially if you are not too sick. Because when you say, "I am sick" everybody wants to help you, giving you lots of treatments and care.

We have to die one day, everybody has to die, everybody who is born, dies. And now it is so nice here [in Europe], every possible facility for treatment is available. If it is really time to die, maybe you will not even be allowed to die, because the facilities that are available now are so good. So, what is there to worry about? And then, as everybody has to die, it's good to die one day. I don't want to be 120 years old and not dying. Not able to move, not able to see, not able to hear, not able to walk and then not dying, that would not be very nice.

His Holiness the Dalai Lama said something once, which really touched me deeply. He was asked, "You always say that everybody has to keep a positive attitude, to be optimistic. Yet your situation is hopeless. The situation of Tibet is hopeless. How can you remain optimistic in this situation?" He replied that the statement is correct; the situation is very bad. In the history of Tibet it has never been so bad as it is now and he also said that there is no use in not accepting it, it must be accepted.

He said, "Our situation is awful, nothing about it is good, it seems to be hopeless. That's why we would have to accept that we are in a hopeless situation. Yet to say, "Oh, we are *so* hopeless, it's finished," that wouldn't help. Just expressing hatred, pain, hopelessness, would not help. We are now in this hopeless situation and now in this situation, what can we do to improve it a little bit? Then he started laughing, and said, "It is so hopeless, that whatever you can do would already be an improvement. So, if anything you can do would be an improvement, do it - concentrate on that." When we are trying to improve a situation, even in any small way, and we focus on that, it is already optimistic, because we are trying to do something to make it better.

When we have a problem, most of it stems from locking onto the difficult aspects of our situation. We see a negative situation, a hopeless situation and then we think, "This cannot happen, this should not happen. Why is this happening?" And we only think like that. We just concentrate on the negative side, without accepting it at all. Then we become unable to think, "What is the next step?" Better that we say, "This is the situation: this situation is here, and just not liking the situation alone is not going to change it. I don't like it, but that is how it is. Whether I like it or not, it is like this."

This understanding is what we mean by "using it as a path." In other words, take that situation, understand that situation and then see what you can do about it. If you cannot do anything, then concentrate on something else. Because there is no use in only worrying, feeling bad or angry, being in anguish, about those things you cannot change.

> *As the strength of this pattern gradually builds up, we will find that just about everything we perceive becomes a cause for attracting unhappiness towards us, and happiness will never get a chance.*

> *If we do not realise that it all depends on the way in which we develop this habit in our mind, and instead we put the blame on external objects and situations alone, the flames of suffering, negative karma, aggression and so on will spread like wildfire, without end. This is called "all appearances arising as enemies."*

> *We should arrive at a very precise understanding that the whole reason why sentient beings in this degenerate age are plagued by so much suffering is because they have feeble power for discerning these things.*

> *Not to be hurt by obstacles created by enemies, illness or harmful influences, does not mean to say that things like sickness can be driven away, and that they will never occur again.*

> *Rather, it simply means that they will not be able to obstruct us from practising on the path. In order for this to happen, we need first to get rid of the attitude of being entirely unwilling to face any suffering ourselves and, second, to cultivate the attitude of actually being joyful when suffering arises.*

The central point regarding using suffering as a path, in relation to the world of our perceptions - the display of dependently-arising appearances - is to understand how we see it and how we respond to this suffering. If we can change our way of responding, if we can take our suffering in a different way, without too much aversion to it, without too much resistance to it - in fact if we can take it in a positive way - that itself becomes a transformation: we don't feel suffering anymore, we feel okay, and therefore there has been a transformation. The text now goes on to describe some methods to train in this.

Dropping the attitude of being unwilling to suffer

The more we are afraid of suffering, the more acute that suffering becomes. That is why the more we are unwilling to face an unpleasant situation because we are afraid of it, the more the fear grows and the more intense the suffering becomes. Somebody who is not afraid is somebody who says, "Whatever happens, it is okay."

To give an example, recently some people in Tibet were publically singing songs on the occasion of His Holiness the Dalai Lama's birthday. There was one girl, Kunga Dolma, and also a young man, who were singing very patriotic songs especially addressed to the Dalai Lama and they were interviewed over the telephone by the "Voice of America" radio station. When Kunga Dolma was asked if she was afraid, she replied that she was not, even though she was aware that there had been a discussion and problems could arise from this action. She said, "I am singing, I am sending this message to my Lama and whatever happens, it will be. There is no problem." Then the interviewer suggested that she might be imprisoned. She said, "I have thought about it and I have made my decision, so whatever they want to do, they can do it. It's okay."

This was a case of someone who was willing to go through suffering and problems. This was not a small thing: she could be tortured, amongst other things. The point is that when we make that kind of decision and we have decided that even if we will have to go through lots of pain and problems, it is okay. Then the fear is not there. When we have this kind of decision, that whatever happens it is okay, then there is no more fear.

Think about all the depression, anxiety and irritation we put ourselves through by always seeing suffering as unfavourable, something to be avoided at all costs. Now, think about two things: how useless this is and how much trouble it causes. Go on reflecting on this repeatedly, until you are absolutely convinced.

We give so much time to concerning ourselves with fear, with worry and anxiety that something might happen to us. This causes us so much suffering. We need to reflect on this. Then we will see that we suffer so much by fearing, by being nervous, being anxious, thinking about how much suffering we might experience and by feeling averse to that.

It is very important to know that reacting in this way, with fear, with anxiety, with so much resistance and aversion to suffering, this itself is causing us suffering. Our 'Not-Wanting-To-Suffer' is one of the biggest causes of our suffering. So, if we really don't want to suffer, at least we can take away that wanting so much not to suffer. If we can do that, that alone will ease a lot of our suffering.

There are so many things we have to go through in life without any choice. We have to grow old, whether we like it or not. We get sick, whether we like it or not. We have to die, whether we like it or not. We have to accept many things that we don't like. We have to let go of things we don't want to let go of. We have to go through so many things in life whether we want to or not – there is no choice, this is life. So, why don't we just go through these things? If we just go through them, it may sometimes be bad and painful, it may sometimes be hard, but at least we only go through it at that time. And at that time when we have this hardship or pain, we have that much pain and hardship, but then it is over, it is limited.

But instead our habit is to think, "Oh, I might have to go through this difficulty, I might have this problem, maybe, maybe not." We are always thinking about all the problems we might or might not go through in the future, so we have suffering, pain and anxiety right now, when nothing is even there. And we carry that on through much of our life. And we amplify it, so that sometimes it becomes much, much bigger in our mind than what really happens. Most of the time, what we really go through is much less hard, when we actually go through it, than what we imagined it would be, before it happened. If we just go through what we have to go through without too much resistance, it is much better. I know this, everyone knows this. Isn't it true?

We may have to go to the dentist, and we think that it will be painful, really painful. But if we say, "Okay, whatever happens, let it happen, it doesn't matter, I have to go through it anyway." Then it is much easier.

So the first step is to understand this point, that our resistance, our unwillingness to go through such things, our aversion to them and our fear of the suffering and problems associated with them, creates much unnecessary suffering for us. That is something that we must know very clearly right from the beginning.

We have to work on accepting this, and these words from the Bodhicharyavatara are very helpful:

'If we can change something, then there is no need to worry and be unhappy about it.
If we cannot change something, then there is no use in being unhappy about it.'

This is an extremely important instruction. Maybe something is going to happen that is not nice, or good, that is painful, something we don't like. If we see that this is not happening now, even though it might happen in the future, we don't need to worry about that now.

What we can do is to look and see if there is anything we can do to prevent the unwanted event, or to alter it. If there is anything that we can do, then we do it. Why worry? Why be unhappy about it? First do whatever you can to make it better. Sometimes there is nothing we can do about it. It will happen, or it is happening. Then what is the use of being worried about it? We may worry about it as much as we like, it doesn't make it better. I think everybody can understand that.

No bad thing that we anticipated ever failed to happen because we worried about it. We will never say that we didn't get sick because we worried so much that we might get sick. The fact is, the more we worry, the more likely it is that this will happen. Worrying, or being afraid, or being unhappy about something, doesn't prevent that thing from happening. There is only one logical way to do that, which is to take the appropriate action that will prevent it – if possible. If not, we have to go through it, and in that case, it's better to go through it lightly, happily, smiling. Because there is no choice.

So, as we try to develop this attitude, we need to try to understand how important this way of facing problems is. When we have this understanding, when we have this resolve: "I will go through it and whatever will happen, I will go through it as nicely and in the best way I can," then at least we don't have the additional pain of our extra anxiety, fear, worry and so on. Also, when we can go through it in that way, in a more positive way, in a more accepting way, then the actual pain is much less; it can also be, even, that there is no pain. This is the first point we need to understand.

Then say to yourself: "From now on, whatever I may have to suffer, I will never become anxious or irritated." Go over this again and again in your mind, and summon all your courage and determination.

Look at how useless it is. If we can do something to solve a problem, then there is no need to worry or be unhappy about; if we can't, then it doesn't help to worry or be unhappy about it either.

As long as we don't get involved in the enormous trouble of getting anxious and irritated, then our strength of mind will enable us to bear even the hardest of sufferings easily; they'll feel as flimsy and insubstantial as cotton wool. But while we are dominated by anxiety, even the tiniest problem becomes extremely difficult to cope with, because we have the additional burden of mental discomfort and unhappiness.

Imagine, for example, trying to get rid of desirous attachment for someone we find attractive, while continuing to dwell all the while on their attractive qualities. It would all be in vain. In just the same way, if we concentrate only on the pain brought by suffering, we will never be able to develop endurance or the ability to bear it. So, as in the instructions called "Sealing the Doors of the Senses," don't grasp onto all kinds of mind-made concepts about your suffering. Learn instead to leave your mind undisturbed in its own natural state; bring it home to rest there and let it find its own ground.

I think this is self-explanatory. The more we worry and remain unready to face whatever has to come, the stronger our problems will seem. The more we face up to them, whatever may come, the lighter they will become. If our general attitude in life is that we do whatever we can to make things better, we are likely to have less suffering, fewer problems.

But in samsara, meaning in our ordinary life, it is not possible to be completely free from problems. There are lots of problems and there is lots of pain and suffering, anyway, everywhere. So therefore we also have to go through all those things that have been described. And when we have to go through them, we *have* to go through them. There is nothing we can do about it. So, it's okay.

We can accept this and decide to make life and its problems as light as possible and go through it in as natural a way as possible, even joyfully. When we make it as light as possible, as natural as possible, we bring our mind to its home. Then, as the text states, there is no need to worry too much and no use in worrying too much. There is no need to have so much anxiety and so much fear, because it doesn't work anyway. So therefore, think, "Whatever may happen, let it happen, I will go through it smiling."

Of course, at the same time we will do our best that everything goes well. In this way, when we are prepared, if small problems come up, they naturally do not create big problems. Because, when we are ready to go through the worst problems, then if small problems come up, they diminish in importance, they lose their significance. It can also happen that when we are ready to go through big problems, then some of those problems no longer seem so big.

It is possible that I could die tonight. There is no guarantee that I will not die tonight. I am not talking only about myself. So therefore if it comes, it comes. What can we do? So we have to be ready. There is no other way. We cannot say: "I am not ready, please excuse me." You cannot say that, it's no use. When our time comes, we have to go through it; we have to face it.

Then, if we are prepared to die today, we think, "If I lose my job, so what? At least I am alive." But if we think, "I have lost my job, how terrible, how can this happen?" then we are not prepared for the higher, bigger and more serious problems of life. Then, if something small happens, it becomes very big in our minds. But if we are prepared for the bigger problems, then if something small happens, we will take it without much concern. This way of looking at things, of dealing with things, is a very important point.

I knew someone who had lost her job and her boyfriend at the same time and, totally devastated by this, was considering committing suicide. I said to her, "You may commit suicide if you want, but first, go to India and spend some time there, and then you can do what you want." She didn't go to India but she went to Japan and she had a very bad accident there. She fell into a pit where nobody could see her. She was alone there and unable to get out, and she thought that she was going to die. But luckily somebody did come and she got out.

Then she came back and when I met her, she was smiling. So I asked her what had happened. She told me, "Oh, it was so great - I nearly died. But I am okay, everything is very nice now." She said that when she fell into the pit and she lost hope of ever getting out, all those problems, losing her job, losing her boyfriend, just disappeared. The only thought in her mind at that time was the wish to live and when she did – how wonderful!

So, this can be our attitude, we can see things in this way. Alternatively, we can take a small problem - like a neighbour that is not so nice - and amplify it, so that it really makes our life miserable. We can take a small thing, even a very small thing, and get upset by it. The size doesn't matter; sometimes people are so affected by such small things. They cannot tolerate them because they think everything should be perfect. This indicates that they are not ready to face life. And we need to be ready to face life. Life, and death, also.

Cultivating the attitude of being joyful when suffering arises

This means that we should not only be ready to go through suffering, but to accept it, to feel joyful and happy, when suffering comes.

> *Seeing suffering as an ally to help us on the path, we must learn to develop a sense of joy when it arises. Yet we need to have some kind of spiritual practice to bring to suffering whenever it strikes, one which matches the capacity of our mind.*
>
> *Otherwise, no matter how many times we might say to ourselves: "If I've got roughly the right method, I'll be able to use suffering and obtain such and such benefit," it's highly unlikely that we'll succeed. We'll be as far from our goal, as the earth is from the sky.*

This is showing us that it's necessary for us to see problems and suffering as allies, as our helpers. For them to function in this way, we need to find a way to take them as a practice, so that we can say to ourselves: " I can use this, I can learn from this, it can benefit me." Then it is okay, it is good, it is wonderful.

When we can see that, then we can really use that suffering as a path. "Now I have suffering, I can use it, so I like it." And then we can even welcome it. When we actually welcome suffering, then we have really transformed it. Because then, when suffering happens, it is no longer suffering.

Do Drupchen advises us that, if we have sorrow or pain, in accordance with our ability, we should directly mix our experience with the practice of doing something positive. If you can carry whatever happens as an inspiration to do positive practice, then it becomes a cause for rejoicing, instead of becoming wearied by it. This means carrying, and a little bit welcoming, whatever injuries we encounter in a positive way.

There was once someone who wanted to take ordination as a monk (I think it was with a Jain master). When he became a monk, he asked his teacher, "I want to practice very strongly, so what should I do?" His teacher told him, "From this day on, pay everybody in the community to insult you. The more they can insult you, the better it will be." So he had to do so. He was paying everyone to insult him, asking them, "Can you insult me for half an hour? I will pay you to do it." This went on for a long time and then one day he went into town. In this town there was a crazy man who was always insulting people and the people there often beat him up for this.

When this monk came along, the crazy man started to insult him, but the monk was so happy that he hugged him and thanked him. This was a genuine shock to the crazy man, because he usually got beaten for insulting people. He said, "I usually get beaten for this, why are you hugging me and thanking me?"

The monk replied, "It is kind of the same for me - usually I have to pay someone to insult me, but you are giving me insults for free!"

If we see something that is usually considered unpleasant or not good, as something that we have to do and also as something that benefits us, then we will like that thing. Then it becomes a source of joy and not of suffering. Then when a problem comes, it is not the source of suffering but it is a source of joy.

What determines whether a problem – somebody insulting us, for example - becomes a source of suffering or a source of joy is how we see it. That is what we need to understand.

Seven methods to train ourselves

Now Do Drupchen Rinpoche describes the seven methods for training in this approach, which are:

1. *Using suffering to train in renunciation*
2. *Using suffering to train in taking Refuge*
3. *Using suffering to overcome arrogance*
4. *Using suffering to purify harmful actions*
5. *Using suffering to find joy in positive action*
6. *Using suffering to train in compassion*
7. *Using suffering to cherish others more than yourself*

1. Using suffering to train in renunciation

Sometimes use your suffering in order to train your mind in renunciation.

Say to yourself: "As long as I wander in samsara, powerless and without any freedom, this kind of suffering is not something unjust or unwarranted. It's simply the very nature of samsara." At times, develop a deep sense of revulsion by thinking: "If it's already so hard for me to bear even the little suffering and pain of the happy realms, then what about the suffering of the lower realms? Samsara really is an ocean of suffering, fathomless and without any end!" Then turn your mind towards liberation, and enlightenment.

To reflect on, and understand, our samsaric state of being is very important. As long as we have this samsaric state of mind, we are going to experience lots of confusion, lots of aggression and lots of greed and attachment. We will do lots of negative things, which bring suffering and pain for ourselves. We will do lots of things which bring problems and suffering to others. We will hurt each other and inflict problems on each other. And we will go through lots of pain and create problems for ourselves.

In this world there are some whose condition is much worse than ours and some whose condition is a little bit better; there is a great diversity. But if we look at our human world, we will see that there have been many bad, negative things happening, throughout all of history. And they still happen. And as long as we have this samsaric state of mind, they will keep on happening. If we look into the animal world, they are all eating each other, it's very scary, it's not at all nice. Look into the oceans and the forests: all the animals are eating each other. That is what it is like; that is samsara.

Within samsara, we human beings claim that we are the best, the most evolved beings. We are supposed to be happy. But we create so many problems, even pain and atrocities, for each other. We are a little bit evolved, but really not so much; our animal instinct is still there. We still want to eat each other. We don't literally bite, but we have that animal instinct. So, as long as we cannot transform this, we will have to continuously face problems and suffering.

We should also know that the problems that we face now, in this life, in our current situation in this society, are comparatively small. When we experience these difficulties, we can take them as a reminder that it is really necessary, not only for ourselves but for everybody else, to transcend this samsaric way of being. So much aggression, so much fear, so much greed, so much dissatisfaction, so much always running after, always running away from things.

So whenever problems appear in our life, this is a reminder that we need to work towards the state of liberation from the samsaric state of being, towards bringing lasting peace and happiness to ourselves and to others. We need to think, "Whatever hardships there may be, whatever problems and pain I may have to go through for however long it may take, I must work for that." Then, we can think: "This little suffering, this little pain is nothing for me. I will make the resolve to go through any kind of pain, of problem, of suffering in order to help myself and all sentient beings to liberate from this state of being."

When you can say that and deeply implant it as your attitude, as your way of looking at life, your problems will become less significant. Because now you have a very important and long-term goal, which requires lots of courage, lots of perseverance and lots of compassion. For example, you may become determined to climb Mount Everest. Then, when you have climbed up a few steps, you will feel this is just the beginning, this is nothing, only a little bit cold. You are ready to do more.

This kind of understanding and determination, that it is very important to take our sufferings, problems and pain as our path is something very useful. And the more problems you have, the more you can be convinced that the suffering arising from these problems is something I have not only to deal with, but uproot. And I have to do this not only for myself, but for everybody else, so therefore these problems are nothing I have to get rid of. To free myself and everybody else from suffering, I must work very hard and go through everything, even hell-realms and things like that. So this is the kind of motivation which is required.

Understanding samsara as well as the samsaric state of mind, is also very important. If you find that you don't have problems, then what is happening? Something must be wrong if it is samsara and there are no problems. Because samsaric people always have a lot of ignorance, we react with lots of aversion, attachment, and ignorance; so there is a lot of suffering and unhappiness. That is the way it is. That is the samsaric state.

The more you understand samsara, the less you expect everybody to be nice and perfect. So when you experience people being not so nice to you, this is normal, this is samsara. If everybody is too kind, then you doubt that is samsara. You ask, "Am I still in this world?" Then you look at your shadow. It is there, I am still in this world (it is said in Tibet that someone who has died no longer has a shadow). If people are too nice, then you say, "Am I still in this world?" So therefore, when you see these problems you can know that this is the nature of samsara. It is the way it is.

Of course we definitely need to slowly transform that, but it is not easy to transform. So therefore it must be accepted. This is the way, to know this and accept it, that this is the samsaric way. You can't find everybody nice, you don't even expect that. You don't expect everything to go well. You don't expect that everything is always successful, good and nice.

Then it is also the samsaric way of things that, even if everything is okay, I am still not very okay. That is the samsaric problem. Everything is okay but I am still not totally satisfied. When everything is okay, nothing is wrong, then I am bored. If I have nothing to complain about, I am bored. If something happens, then I am overwhelmed. So I am never satisfied. Whatever happens, I am never satisfied. That is samsara.

Nirvana is the opposite: whatever may go wrong, I am okay. That's it. Therefore if you find you can take samsara in a nice way, then that itself is Nirvana. This transformation is a very difficult thing to do because our reactive habits are very strong. Yet in one way it's very simple. It is just a matter of slightly changing the way we react, nothing more than that. It is not that it happens very easily, it needs a lot of practice, lots of understanding and lots of perseverance. But fundamentally it is nothing too difficult, nothing too complicated. To understand that is very important.

2. Using suffering to train in taking Refuge

Say to yourself: "Life after life, again and again we are continuously plagued by these kinds of fear, and the one and only protection that can never fail us is the Three Jewels: the precious guide, the Buddha; the precious path, the Dharma; and the precious companions on the way, the Sangha. So it is on them that I must rely, entirely. Whatever happens, I will never renounce them." Let this become a firm conviction, and train in the practice of taking refuge.

When there is some understanding that there is a possibility to transform, to transform myself, and also others, then I can go for refuge. In taking the Buddha as a refuge, there is the possibility for me to be free from any kind of suffering and really have lasting peace and happiness.

Secondly, because there is a path, there is a way to do this and so I am able to completely commit myself to working on that path, through the use of different practices and methods. The more I see the suffering, pain and problems of samsaric life, the more I become determined to work to transform that. It makes me more enthusiastic to work on the path.

When difficulties arise, I try not to say, "Oh, this is so bad, why is this happening to me, now I am just going to have to give up." Not like that. Try to see that problems are something that happen for everybody. When I am sick, I try to understand that I am not the only one who gets sick - everybody gets sick. If negative problems fall on me, it is not just my experience, these things happen to everyone.

So, as long as I have not completely transformed my attitude and attained Buddhahood, I will keep on taking refuge. There is no use in being afraid of, or so touchy about, little problems. We have to go on our path whatever happens. So we should make ourselves clearer, more diligent, more determined in working towards transformation. If I am totally committed to this, nothing can put me down. If you use taking refuge and your practice in this way - so clear, so important, so personal - then, whatever problems come, you just have to overcome them. You have no time to get obsessed with problems; problems keep on coming, so what? And if you really understand that, those problems become the path.

Then, when problems come, if I become angry, for example, when somebody is not so nice to me, I can say, "Oh, that's really good, because this is something I can use to practice on." I can be happy that there is something not so good, because then there is something I can work on - that is the Dharma. What is Dharma practice? It is none other than, when there is something like an obstacle or a problem, to work on it. There are many great masters who have taught this kind of understanding.

There was a Sufi master who had had someone in his group who was very nasty. He was always causing lots of problems for everybody because of his unpleasant talk and constant criticism. For example, every time the master said something that person always contradicted it. Then he passed away and when this happened everybody was rather happy. But when they came to their master, they found that he was crying profusely. They asked him, "What is wrong with you? This man made so much trouble, you should be really happy." The master replied, "It's not like that. He was my main source of practice. He taught me so many things, and through him I learned so much. He was my real friend who dared to contradict me. It is my greatest loss."

If we could be like that when someone is not so nice to us, it would be very good. Maybe someone can object to your brilliant ideas, or they can tell you that you are fat and old. Nobody tells me that here. When I went back to Sikkim I was surprised. Everybody I met said, "Oh, you are so fat, you are so old." It was not said with any bad intention: "You became so old!" Maybe that is just the Tibetan way. When my uncle went to Bodhgaya, he met an old friend he had not seen for many years. Uncle said, "Oh, you look so old." The other one said, "What are you saying to me? You yourself are looking like a momo, and then you are saying I have become old!" - A momo is a kind of Tibetan dumpling or pastry, which is all wrinkled!

3. Using suffering to overcome arrogance

As I explained before, (as long as we are in samsara) we are never independent or truly free or in control of our lives. On the contrary, we are always at the mercy of suffering. So we must eliminate "the enemy that destroys anything that is wholesome and good" which is arrogance and pride; and we must do away with the evil attitude of belittling others and considering them as inferior.

So, when we fail to achieve our goals, when we do not get things that we want, or we get things we don't want, and so on, then we can understand that that is also a lesson. We can think, "The more I have pride and arrogance, the more I will get hurt when things don't happen as I wish." So we can therefore say, "This is nothing to feel hurt about, nothing to feel pain about, because it is just the way things are. And I am happy that my pride, my arrogance, is a little bit dented by this. So, thank you very much, I am happy to soften my pride a little bit."

Sometimes we think, "I am so good that everybody should like me, everybody should do as I say, everybody should love me, and everybody should say good things about me." When some people don't do this, then we are shocked. Why is that? At that time, remind yourself: "This is a good thing for me. It helps me to control my pride a little bit, my unnecessary pride and arrogance."

4. Using suffering to purify harmful actions

Remind yourself of this realisation: "All the suffering, which I'm going through, and other suffering which is greater still – all the boundless suffering that there is – comes from nothing but harmful, negative actions."

Reflect, carefully and thoroughly, on the following:

Four reasons for this are given according to the Buddhist point of view:

1. *The action of karma is certain – causes unfailingly produce their results.*
   Whatever kind of seeds you sow as a cause, that kind of fruit will grow. So therefore, whatever kind of action you do, that kind of experience or result is what you will have. That is what we call karma.
2. *Karma multiplies enormously.*
   If you do something very negative, that will tend to become your habitual way of being, your tendency. If being hurt, or being angry, or being sad becomes your habit; that is very likely to increase and grow more and more over time.
3. *You will never face the effects of something you have not done.*
   It is not possible to have a result unless there was previously an action, or some kind of a condition that you have created as the cause.
4. *Whatever you have done will never go to waste.*
   If you perform a negative action, there will be a negative result and, equally, a positive action will produce a positive result.

Here, we are not talking only about actions of the body, but also those of speech and mind – those involving emotions and intentions. When you perform some action with a strong intention, it will result in a strong imprint on yourself.

So if you had a problem, if you had to go through a difficult situation or experience, then you can know that this is the result of your own experiences, actions and reactions of the past. Therefore we can say, "I cannot blame anybody, I have to work on it myself. I have to change, to purify, the habitual tendencies from the past."

Then we have to create a positive way of being, positive habitual tendencies, positive ways of reacting. If some negative problem or pain comes to us, then we can say, "That is fine, this is the result of my previous negative actions." Then we can decide to use this present situation to purify those previous actions and not to react in the same way, but in a more positive way. In this way we will become able to use the resultant suffering to purify the negative deeds that caused it. Then we can think, "By experiencing this problem or this suffering, may I be able to get rid of all my negative actions, karma. Not only mine, but, as with the practice of Tonglen, may this be able to eliminate the negative karmas and negative actions of all other beings."

When I can say this, when I can deeply feel this, then I will not be so unhappy. I can be happy that I am willing to use these problems and their pain to purify, so that, as a result, I do not have them again. So this is the method of using suffering as purification.

The following important point arises from this: sometimes, people say: "We see this person is suffering, we should let him suffer, because this process will cause him to get rid of his suffering, so we should not get involved, we should not interfere, just let him suffer."

That is not right, that is not the Buddhist way of thinking. If somebody is suffering and we can help, we should help, we should reduce their suffering. Suffering alone will not get rid of negative karma. Suffering can create more negative karma, because when we suffer we usually have negative reactions to that. We get angry, we get upset, and then more negative emotions arise. The text is not suggesting this response at all.

If you can go through suffering and say, "I use this to let go of all my negative karma, I use it as a means to develop purification," then that is okay. In this case you are using the pain and problems you are having as a means to purify and remove negative karma, so therefore you are looking at these problems as being a purification process. When you are looking at something not-so-nice as a purification process, or as something that you can learn from, or that you can use as a kind of challenge, it becomes an incentive to do something more positive. Then it becomes positive. That is what the text is talking about.

> *Then say to yourself: "So, if I really don't want to suffer any more, then I must give up the cause of suffering, which is negativity." With the help of the Four Powers, make an effort to acknowledge and purify all the negative actions you have accumulated in the past, and then firmly resolve to avoid doing them in the future.*

5. Using suffering to find joy in positive action

> *Say to yourself: "If I really want to find happiness, which is the opposite of suffering, then I have got to make an effort to create its cause, which is positive action." Think about this in detail and from every angle, and dwell on the implications. Then in every way possible, do whatever you can to increase your positive, beneficial actions.*

When you know that previously occurring negative causes and conditions which you created are the reason why you presently experience painful negative experiences, you will understand that if you don't like such painful experiences and you don't want them, you need to change. You need to cultivate a more positive way of being: kindness, compassion, doing something that would help others. You need to base your actions on all the positive qualities that you would like to have.

With this understanding of karma, you can see that if you have a negative state of mind, a painful one, a suffering one, one that is not-so-nice, that means you need to change it. There is no use saying, "I cannot do it." That is just an excuse and there *is* no excuse. Because, if you really don't want to have this kind of suffering, you need to change.

So therefore you need to find ways and means to transform your actions, to increase the opposite, the positive, qualities. In order to consider the negative actions of our body, speech and mind, we have to look at ourselves and say: "What is it that I am doing? How is it that I am thinking? How is it that I am reacting? Am I reacting in a negative way? Am I reacting to everything that is happening to me, to whatever somebody is doing or saying, with anger, with pride, with jealousy, with negative actions of body and speech?" If I am behaving in that way and then I get the same negative actions from everybody, then that's very good. I deserve what I am getting, because, this is the way I am acting, so I must get that. So I got what I wanted. So it's very good. If I throw a stone in the sky, of course it will fall on my head. So you get what you want. That's very nice, because I got what I wanted. So if I don't want it, I don't need to do that, I should not do it. I should react in a different way. So therefore I should watch myself - how I am reacting, how I am taking things, how I am acting with my body, speech and mind. And then I should do the opposite.

Even if somebody says something a little bit unpleasant, you can reply a little bit more nicely. Then see what happens. If he or she again says something not very nice, you reply again very nicely. Do it three or four times and see what happens. I think this person will like you very much for it. It's natural, that is the way it is. Sometimes it is very difficult to change things, but sometimes just small things can make a big change.

What response you make to any situation you may be in, how you take things moment by moment, affects your life. Life is lived moment by moment; what happens depends on how I act and react, moment by moment. So therefore it is very important that we work with our present situation. With simple things, of course. We cannot completely transform ourselves in an instant.

I might suddenly have a very big problem and then say, "Now I am doing it, I am transforming my perception." But it does not happen like that: I can't only assert through words that I am practising Dharma. For example, if you break your leg and in the morning you might say: "Now I am practising Dharma, I am getting rid of my pain. I like this pain very much." You can't like this pain very much. So therefore in the afternoon you say, "Dharma practice is useless, because I cannot get rid of this pain coming from my broken leg."

It doesn't work like that, that is not how to do it. First you start with small things: for example, if somebody comes to you with a little bit of a serious face, then you can try a smile, or say something positive. Then see what happens. Then you can slowly increase these sorts of positive responses.

Normally we only see problems. We say, "This is a problem, that is a problem, that is a problem, this is a problem." I know somebody who was a trouble-shooter for big companies running oil rigs. He told me that once he visited twenty or thirty oil rigs, then everybody came together to meet and discuss the situation. He was observing, he was not saying anything. So through his observation, he noticed that they were collecting all the problems: "This rig has this problem, this rig has that problem, let us discuss these problems." So they were discussing their problems and trying to solve them, but they were not solving them. Then he noticed that there were one or two oil rigs where there were no problems. They ran very well, but nobody took any notice of them, because they had no problems.

Then he asked to go to the places where there were no problems - he had previously only been sent to the places where there were problems.

When he went to those well-functioning rigs, he tried to find out why they had no problems and he found out exactly what they were doing that was different from the others. He very quickly learned why they didn't have problems: they were doing their work very positively. So he said, "Let's try looking at what these people were doing who had no problems, instead of talking about the problems." That then became the focus of the next series of meetings, which were suddenly totally changed. My friend said that everybody brightened up, everything changed and the meetings became very effective.

In the same way, when things are going well in our own lives we don't care - we don't really notice it. But when just one thing doesn't go well, we concentrate fully on it, and we become unhappy. Of course we should not ignore what is not going well; but, as we said before, sometimes difficulties, these things which are not so nice for us, can also be used as a means to enhance our positive side. When we practice using our suffering to find joy in positive action, we can look at the positive things going on in our lives and think, "This life is much nicer than I thought it was, when I see that there are all these positive things about which I can be happy, I can see that it could be worse. It could be much worse, so it's not too bad." There are many different ways in which we can view our lives. And of course, how bad things seem usually depends on how bad you let your view of the situation be. If you say, "Oh, it's really so bad, it's completely impossible," then it will tend to become like that.

I recently saw an advertisement in India in which a young woman found a white hair on her head. She started crying to her mother: "Look! I have white hair, my life is finished. What can I do?" Then they gave her a special kind of hair dye and she cheered up. She said: "This is my last white hair." As if, even with one white hair, you can think, "My life is finished." And many times we react like that. Something happens and then we think, "This is the end, it's finished." But it is not finished. Life is not like that.

There is a story I tell about a very jolly Lama who lives in Denmark. He didn't go to Denmark as a Lama, but just to work as a manual labourer. One day one of his colleagues said to him, "Goodbye, see you in the next life. I am going to commit suicide." Then the conversation went like this:

"What! Why are you committing suicide?"

"Well, I don't like all this work too much, my boss is not nice, and my wife is leaving me. So I am committing suicide."

"So, your wife is leaving you, and you are committing suicide? Is there only one woman in the world?"

"No, there are many. Actually this is not my first marriage. This is my third marriage."

"Then why didn't you commit suicide when your first marriage ended?"

"The first time, I left her."

"Then why didn't you commit suicide the second time?"

"The second time, we both decided to separate."

"Well, you already separated twice and you got another wife. So, if you separate this time also, you might get another one. But think it over. If you really think it's the last time then, of course you can go ahead with your plan, but I don't think you need to see it like that. You should think properly before you commit suicide. Because you cannot reverse it."

After a few days his colleague came and said, "Yes, you were right. I decided not to commit suicide." Then he said, "You are very strange, every time I come here, you always have the same stable, peaceful mood. What do you do? How do you manage it?"

The Lama answered: "Why not? Why should I be in different moods all the time? I am not forced to be here. I asked for a job. They gave me a job. I am doing my job and I am paid. So I don't have anything to be unhappy about."

Then his colleague said, "Yes, that is true. Maybe I would like to become a Buddhist like you."

The Lama replied, "Maybe it's good to do something, to learn something about Buddhism and practise some meditation. But it is not necessary to become a Buddhist. I can talk to you about these things." But he did not speak the language very well. So they got a translator and slowly, gradually, the colleague changed. After some time another of his colleagues came to him similarly and both of them became changed.

Then the boss said, "What did you do to these people? Do it to me also!" So, it started like that.

Sometimes it's just our way of seeing things that causes us problems. We have variable moods, we are up today and down tomorrow. I think it is because there is something wrong with our attitude. If we had a different way of looking at things, we would not be like that.

One day very happy, one day very unhappy – always changing. This doesn't happen if we learn to practise a little bit. It is very important to reflect on these things and not only to think about them, but also to use the methods that the teachings explain to us. You should read and you should reflect. Because it is about the way you see things.

How we see things, how we look at things, is very important. We need to look at how we are always reacting. Emotions are temporary, yet we always think they are not. We say, "I like this. I don't like that. I feel like this." When you say, "I feel good," you say it as if it is like this all the time. But it's not like that. By the evening it has changed. So that means emotions are not so important. Because they change all the time. I may want something very much, yet it is really not so important. Because by tomorrow, maybe I don't want it anymore. If I strongly don't want to have something, that is also not so important. After some time, that also changes. Our emotions are like the Irish weather.

For those who have not been to Ireland, the weather there changes a lot. The Irish themselves say that if you like it, then wait five minutes, if you don't like it, wait five minutes. But they take it very nicely. Once a tourist went there and asked a shepherd, "What do you think the weather will be like today?"

He replied, "It will be exactly as I like it."

After some time it started to rain really heavily. The tourist said, "You said it would be as you like it, but it's so bad…"

"But this is how I like it," the shepherd replied.

Then, if you don't mind change, change is no problem. Maybe we can take emotions in this way. If we are a little upset, so what? After some time it will go. Or, if I am little angry, so what? If I am a little sad, so what? If I am a little excited, so what? It is all okay. Because after some time it will change. So, therefore, it is no big deal. We can have that view, we can understand that we don't have to be so nervous, so excited, so overwhelmed by emotions. If I am a little bit sad, that's it. I am a little sad. So what? I do not need to be totally overwhelmed.

The alternative is that we think, "If I am sad, that is terrible - how can I be sad? I must do something to stop myself being sad. I must drink wine; I must smoke a cigarette; I must find a friend; I must talk to somebody. Why doesn't everybody come to me and talk to me and console me and make me feel better?" Then actually it becomes worse and worse, because things don't improve like that. But if I don't mind, if I say, "It is okay," then it becomes okay. So this way of seeing things is very important.

There are different ways to train our mind so that we can transform suffering, that which we don't like, into something which we don't have too much aversion to, or something that we can even be happy to accept. These are the methods for transforming suffering into the path, and the next one is:

6. Using suffering to train in compassion

Our compassion is based on the understanding that "I don't want to suffer and everybody else is like me, so they also would not like to have pain, suffering and problems." So, therefore, when I see, or when I feel, that somebody else is having problems or pain, I can wish that this isn't happening. I wish, or I want to do something, so that the suffering of others is relieved or changed, transformed into something better. Thus understanding compassion comes from the understanding of suffering.

When we have such an understanding, we will become concerned. We can become very clear that we would not only like to transform our own suffering, but to work for the elimination of the suffering of all beings. And when we see how many problems, how much pain, how many difficulties there are here in the world, this awareness diminishes our own problems. The more compassion you have, the more you can see the problems of others everywhere in the world and the more you become concerned about their welfare - especially if you really wish to do something about that - the lesser your own problems become. And you also become happier generally.

People who are compassionate and altruistic, who want to work for the benefit of others or are very concerned about others, are usually happier people. They tend to be more easy-going in themselves and less sensitive to their own small problems.

If they can overlook little problems they can become more patient. If I am only thinking about myself, then when somebody is a little upset or angry or annoyed with me, I will think, "What did I do that he has become so upset?" I can develop much unhappiness about that.

But perhaps we can see the possibility that the reason someone is upset, or angry, or speaking or acting in not so nice ways is because he or she is unhappy, experiencing problems or pain and so on of their own.

When I can see this, my understanding of their behaviour changes. It doesn't annoy me anymore because I can see their suffering.

I know a story about a traveller on a train. He had had a bad day, so he was feeling very tense and irritable when another man came in to his compartment with two small children. These children were not really behaving very nicely. They were running around and making lots of noise and generally being naughty. And their father was doing nothing. So the first passenger became really upset. He thought, "Why is this man not even saying one word to his children when they are doing so many things that are disturbing other people?" He was getting really agitated and angry.

Then, at some point, the father of the children said to him, "I am very sorry that the children are like this, but they just lost their mother and I don't know what to do with them." Immediately the first passenger, who had been very upset and angry just moments before, totally changed his attitude. He had a different way to look at the situation. Before, when he didn't know the whole story, he thought, "This father is not looking after his children, he is not giving them any discipline." Then, when he heard their story he immediately understood the big suffering behind their behaviour and so his reaction was totally different.

When we understand people, when we see their suffering and their problems, then compassion naturally arises. Your reaction to problems that arise changes – you react differently. So I think it is very important to try to look from this point of view. The root text says:

> *Say to yourself: "Just like me, others too are tormented by suffering that is similar, or even much worse than mine." Train yourself to generate the thought: "If only they could be free from all this suffering, how wonderful that would be!" This will also help you to understand how to practice loving kindness, where the focus of the practice is for those who have no happiness.*

7. Using suffering to cherish others more than yourself

This means offering your own happiness in exchange for the problems of others. The point to be understood is this: Why are we unhappy? The main reason is that we have so much aversion to unhappiness. I like being happy, and I want to get happiness for myself, too much. Therefore when that wish is not fulfilled I become very unhappy. Then my holding on to cherishing happiness for myself becomes the main cause for my unhappiness. I run after happiness so much, I crave so much to be happy, I am so attached to happiness and joy. If that attachment to happiness was not there, then I would not be unhappy.

This is a very important point and it is difficult to understand. We think, "I must be happy, what is there that can make me happy? I must do something to make myself happy." And then I am not so happy. I am not so happy and I think it is really bad that I am not so happy. And then a little bit of something nice happens: "Oh, that's very good, now I am going to be happy." And when that is finished, then I am still not happy. The more I crave happiness, the more I expect to be happy or entertained, the more unhappy and bored I actually become.

I discovered boredom in America - where the conditions were all basically very good. At that time in Sikkim we didn't have television. Or, if we did have television, there were just a few government channels, which only showed programmes about how to plant vegetables and so on (now, of course, there are many more). So, I was in America and I did not have much work I had to do; I just had to give two classes a week. So I had all this time. I could sit in front of the television, with hundreds of channels available, with the remote control in my hand.

So, I was looking at the television, thinking, "I am going to enjoy myself here." I started going up, up, up, through one hundred and twenty channels and then back down, down, down. And after some time, I found myself to be not really very happy at all. I wondered what was going on. Then suddenly I realised: this is what they call boredom! Boredom is a very interesting thing. It is a feeling of dissatisfaction, based on the wish to be satisfied or entertained. We think, "There is no reason why I should not be entertained." So when life is not entertaining, we become a little bit angry, a little bit upset.

This is the same point we were looking at earlier. The more I want, the more I wish or expect to be happy, the more it doesn't happen. When I know that it's not possible to be totally satisfied in a samsaric state of mind, it is therefore okay when I am not totally satisfied, or completely entertained. When I don't expect that, then I am happier. I can say, "It is okay, it could be worse." Therefore, when it is the case that my own too-much-wishing, too-much-wanting to be happy is the source of my unhappiness and dissatisfaction, I realise that I need to change that way of seeing things. I understand that I cannot be totally satisfied and that is okay. Then I can look to see if I can do something that would give a little help to others who are suffering, who have more problems than they can handle. Because, even if I am a little bit entertained for a while, it doesn't last anyway, so it's no use. I will not be made totally happy and joyful by such enjoyment.

Instead, I can look to see if I can do something to help other people, to benefit them, even in a small way. Even if it is little bit hard to do, it's okay, it's worth it. I can say: "I will do this." I find that this is what we should do.

Many young people say to me, "I would like to find a good profession for myself, I want to do something that is really interesting to me." I tell them that that is the wrong way of looking at it. Something may be very interesting now, but if it is done for one year, two, three, four or five years, then it doesn't remain so interesting anymore. And if you take something as your work, it will not remain very interesting anyway.

Something which you are not compelled to do as a job, which you can do in your free time as you like, can remain interesting and satisfying. But if it becomes your work, even something enjoyable like sport will not remain interesting.

So I tell them, "You will lose interest in your profession sometimes." So then they ask me what they can do. I suggest they try to look for something that they find would be really beneficial, helpful to lots of people. And if you choose something like that as your work, even if you are not so interested in it, at least you feel there is some meaning in it. It is not like, "Aaah, every moment I am doing something so interesting, so exciting" but, at the end of the day, you feel you have done something worthwhile and that will inspire you more in the long run. That is very important because when we do something in our life that we think has a purpose, is of benefit to other people, then we feel we have done something useful and meaningful. We feel we have not wasted the day and therefore we can get some satisfaction out of that. And that satisfaction is greater than anything we can find in doing something just for ourselves.

Anyway, when I eat chocolate or ice cream, which I like a lot, it's very nice at the time, but afterwards it is not nice anymore. After eating, the pleasure is finished and maybe by evening I would even think, "Why did I do that? I should have tried to stick to my diet and slowly reduce my weight." Then there is nothing good, nothing enjoyable that remains for tomorrow.

Instead, I could do something to help somebody else. Perhaps I might give something to a beggar on the street. Even though I might not feel so good about my generosity at that time - I might think, "Ah, I could have used the money to buy an ice cream" for example - afterwards I feel a little bit better. I did something good, I gave at least one Euro to somebody. I can think, "On this occasion I was generous." Usually I am not; when I go around with my uncle he always gives somebody something. And I don't, and he gets very annoyed with me. He says, "You are wearing this robe and you are so uncompassionate." It is true. But doing something for others, something that is beneficial, is actually good for me. It gives me greater satisfaction than doing something for myself, in the end.

It is an important point to understand that making efforts to help others will make your own life happier. When you are really thinking about helping others, you don't have much time to get depressed.

Once when I was teaching, two of the people who were present became very upset, to the extent that they were crying the whole day. One of them came up to me and said that they felt really hurt because they had understood me to be saying that they were depressed because they were not compassionate. I did not say that. I did not mean to imply that there is a causal connection like that. Only that training ourselves to help others, increasing our compassion, is one of the ways to work with our mind and it will lift our mood.

There is a story I often tell about someone who had to use a wheelchair and felt quite depressed because of this. Then one day she met someone whose legs had been amputated – he just had stumps covered in leather – and was dragging himself about on the ground on a piece of wood. This man was very joyful and happy, making jokes and so on, so when the lady in the wheelchair saw this, she was very moved. She thought, "If he can be so happy and cheerful, why can't I? I want to do something about that." From that day on, she decided to do at least one thing each day to help somebody else. Since then, she said, she became so busy thinking about what she could do for others that she never had time to feel depressed, or desperate, or lonely. She says this has completely changed her life.

So the way to transform unhappiness into happiness is to work with the way you react. It is not about how things are. You could be very wealthy, with everything going very well and all the conditions of your life perfect, and still you could be very unhappy. Yet, sometimes, everything could be going completely wrong and you could still be happy. It is the way you see things which makes the difference.

Train yourself to think in this way: "The reason why I am not free from suffering is that from time immemorial I have cared only about myself. Now, from this moment onwards, I will only cherish others, as this is the source of all happiness and goodness."

It is extremely difficult to begin using suffering as the path when it has already struck, and is staring us in the face. That is why it is crucial to become familiar with the practices to be used when misfortune and difficulties befall us. It is also particularly helpful, and will really count, if we use the practice we know best, and of which we have a clear, personal experience.

With this understanding, suffering and difficulties can become a help for our spiritual practice - but that alone is not enough. We need to gain a sense of real joy and enthusiasm, inspired by a thorough appreciation for our achievement, and then to reinforce this, and make it stable and continuous.

We need to develop a clear understanding about what is happening and what we are doing. We should know that we are not going to immediately become joyful and happy the first time we do something to help someone else. It's not like that. But little by little, you can learn not to allow your problems or suffering, or unhappiness to totally overcome you. When you first develop a different way of looking at things, little by little, that is already a big deal.

We cannot expect too much. We cannot expect too much from anything. Neither from ourselves, nor from others, nor from the teachings, nor from the teachers. Otherwise it is not going to work. Sometimes people think, "I have studied Dharma, I have meditated for the last one and a half years, but still I don't feel so good." Or they even say, "Why don't you tell me exactly how to be free from suffering? Why don't you?" Maybe it is because I don't know. Even if I knew, this kind of thing cannot be 'told.' It is like that.

I think most of you know how to ride a bicycle, for example. I don't know how to ride a bicycle. I never learnt because I live in the Himalayas. I tried to ride a scooter once. It is not an experience I want to repeat. Because I don't have any balance, I can only go very fast. If I go fast, I am okay, I stay on the scooter. But if I go slowly, then I fall off. So, of course, I kept falling down. To be balanced on a bicycle and not fall off is impossible for me. How can you balance on such a thing?! Anyone would fall down immediately, surely? Tell me exactly how to balance. Who is the best bicycle rider? - Tell me exactly how to do it.

Whatever you tell me, however, I don't think that will make me able to balance. I have to practise or exercise the skill myself. I have to learn for myself. Of course, what you tell me may be useful. But your telling me will not make me immediately able to balance. That is not enough, only my own training can do that. Anything that is practical has to be learned by *doing*, has to be learned by yourself. It cannot be taught. In a way it has to be taught, but in another way it cannot be taught. It is both very easy and very complicated at the same time. So, therefore, we need to learn step by step. We need to exercise, exercise, exercise. You have to fall many times, and get some bruises. Then one day, maybe you will be surprised to find that you have found your balance.

Question: Karma

Student: I have a question about using suffering to purify harmful actions, and how people use the concept of karma to judge others. I knew a woman who went to a therapist and told him she had been abused at some point in her life, it was a revelation for her to be able to speak about this. But the therapist told her, "If that is the case, then in this life you are the victim, but in previous lives you may have been the perpetrator, or something similar to that." That was quite shocking for her.

I thought that karma was not about judging others, but that it was about working with circumstances. What is your opinion on this, and about how people should react to being a victim of abuse and so on?

Rinpoche: This is a total misunderstanding of karma. Some people don't comprehend karma according to the Buddhist understanding. It is a prevalent misunderstanding to say that if someone is suffering, you should let that person suffer, because then they are purifying karma. Therefore you should not involve yourself, you should not interfere in the purification of the karma. Some people in the West - and it is only in the West - say this. And it is a total misunderstanding of karma.

But you can work with karma as a practice for yourself. Everything arises from causes and conditions. And karma is nothing other than the law of cause and effect. The whole of Buddhist philosophy is based on understanding cause and effect, and how they interdependently arise. Since everything is interdependently arising, and everything depends on causes and conditions, there is nothing that happens without a cause. Causes and conditions are what make things happen. Yet the things that happen are not something concrete or solid. Causes and conditions are always making another set of causes and conditions. When a set of causes and conditions arises for a person in relation to an experience; that is called karma.

If something is my karma, it doesn't mean it is my fault. This is something very important to understand. 'My karma' doesn't mean 'my fault.' Karma means: the way I am now is because of what happened to me in the past. Not that I intentionally created the cause of my present condition, that I wanted to be like this, so therefore I did various things and therefore it is my fault. It is not like that.

The way I am now is caused by everything which has happened to me so far and that is what makes me what I am now. My body, my speech, my mind, my personality, the way I react, the way I experience everything, this is my karma. This is a great accumulation of causes and conditions and it is also changeable. The way I am is already the way I am, so I cannot totally or immediately change, because these are causes and conditions that have already occurred. If I want to become a blond German girl tomorrow, for example, it is not possible, because I am already the fat Tibetan man you see before you. But I can change gradually. I have many different characteristics and it is not necessary to change all of them. Some things are more useful and beneficial to change and some things I should be able to change very easily: the way I react to things for instance.

I am an old, fat Tibetan monk. That does not change. But I can become a happy, jolly, old, fat Tibetan monk, or a grumpy, depressed, unhappy old, fat Tibetan monk. That is my choice. So, if we change our attitude, in a way, that is also changing our karma. In terms of karma, the emphasis is more on how I experience what happens and not so much on events themselves. Events themselves depend on many different kinds of causes and conditions, some of them to do with me and some of them not to do with me.

For example, I may have been abused as a child; or I might have gone through many different kinds of experiences. But, whatever has happened in the past, I can say now, "Okay, if I was abused, I was abused. But that is gone now, that is finished. Why should I be so unhappy that I was abused ten years ago, now?" I don't need to be so unhappy because something happened ten years ago.

You can go through an experience and you can come out of it in two ways. You can come out of it and continue to carry it with you, "I am the abused one, I am the abused one..." You identify with the abuse, and so you are 'the abused one.' Then nothing can change anything for you, because you *are* the abused one. And all your life you may remain 'the abused one.' But you can also go through a difficult and painful situation and come out of it saying, "That was a difficult time, that was a horrible thing which happened, but at last I am out of it. Yes, I was abused, but that is now gone. I am not the abused one. I am myself. Something unpleasant, something very bad, happened to me, but that is it."

This is my personal understanding; I think that looking at things in this way can help. The way I look at what happened in the past can change my way of being now. It is not that Buddhists say, "If you were abused, then that is now finished," we don't say it like that. From the Buddhist point of view we say, "I was abused, but I am not the abused one." You should not identify yourself as the abused. If you do that, it creates difficulties. Better to say, you were abused at one time and now that is finished. Now you are just yourself. You do not need to identify yourself all your life as someone who was abused. Everybody goes through many difficulties, many problems, sometimes many kinds of abuse or even many kinds of atrocities. But none of these mean that is who you are.

That is the essence of understanding purification in Buddhism - that you are not the bad guy. Maybe you have done bad things. The way the story develops is like this: a child spills some milk and someone says, "You are a bad child, you have spilled milk." Then the child thinks, "I am a bad child, I have spilled milk." Then you cannot change it. You cannot purify it because, "I am the bad guy because I did that."

But we could say it differently: "You spilled the milk, you didn't do a good thing, you did a bad thing, but you are not a bad child." You just did one bad thing, spilling the milk. If you don't spill more milk, you are no longer doing bad things. From the Buddhist point of view any negative thing is like that. All the negative actions I did, anything negative that happened to me, is something that I did, or something that happened to me. That's why, if I don't do it anymore, I purify it. If I don't cling to it anymore, I purify it. So, the sense of purification is that I can let go.

But if I identify completely with that as myself, there is no way to purify it, because I am 'the bad man,' I am 'the sinner,' I am 'the unhappy one.' If you say, "I am the unhappy one," what can anybody do? Nobody can do anything for me now because, "I am the unhappy one." But if I say, "I feel unhappy now," that is another matter. If I can feel unhappy now, even in the next moment I can feel happy. I can feel angry now, yet in the next moment this can also change. So, therefore, whatever happens, whatever I have done, it is an action, which can be changed, and which does change.

But the real way I am is something different. 'Buddhanature' is what I really am: I am emptiness. I am clarity. I am continuously manifesting. All these actions I have done, or that have happened to me, none of them affect me in my core. They influence me, but they don't make me what I am. That is the general understanding.

———

So, going back to our discussion of the methods to train ourselves, the text goes on:

> *In relation to each of the practices outlined above, say to yourself, this suffering has been of tremendous assistance. It will help me to achieve the many kinds of (temporary) happiness and bliss, which are experienced in the higher realms, and then (permanent) liberation from samsara; these things are extremely difficult to find. From now on too, I know that whatever suffering lies in store for me will have the same potential. So, however tough, however difficult the suffering may be, it will always bring me the greatest joy and happiness. Bitter, yet sweet, like those Indian cakes made of sugar mixed with cardamom and pepper.*

> *Develop this way of thinking over and over again, very thoroughly, so that you accustom yourself to the happy state of mind that it brings. If we reflect in this way, our minds will become so suffused with happiness that the suffering we*

feel through our senses will become almost imperceptible and incapable of disturbing our minds. This is the point at which sickness can be overcome through forbearance. It is worth noting that this is also an indication that difficulties brought about by enemies, harmful spirits and so on may be overcome.

As we have already said, reversing the attitude of not wanting to suffer is the whole basis for integrating the experience of suffering with our spiritual path. This is because we simply won't be able to turn suffering into the path as long as anxiety and irritation continue to eat away at our confidence and disturb our mind.

The more we succeed to actually take suffering onto our path, the more we will enhance and reinforce all our previous practice. This is because our courage and good humour will grow all the more, once we can see from our own experience how suffering causes our spiritual practice and good qualities to blossom. By training gradually in smaller sufferings step by step, in easy stages, then in the end we will be able to handle big sufferings and difficulties too. We must go about it like this, because it is extremely difficult to deal with an experience of something that is beyond our level, or capacity.

I have already pointed out the basic reason we develop unhappiness. It is based on our having so much aversion to something happening which we think is bad, or negative, or painful, or a cause of suffering. We dislike it too much, we wish to get rid of it too much and that creates suffering. If we can find something useful, something we can almost want, in an unpleasant experience, as well as the unpleasantness, that can transform our experience into something that is not unhappy. Then it becomes something that can give us a purpose, that can give us some meaning, which we can learn from. Or something that will be more able to give a fruitful, beneficial, purposeful result, a sweet result, afterwards and in the long run. So this is the way to turn. And also towards understanding that the more we don't like some unpleasant experience, the more we are bothered by the suffering of it, the more suffering we are likely to feel.

Therefore we make it a point that we should not succumb to feelings of aversion. Even if we cannot find anything good in a particular problem or painful experience at the time we have to endure it, there are many other things in our life that we can think about or engage in, that would bring us more purpose, be of more use, bring us more benefit. Instead of focusing all our energy and all our attention on any particular pain or problem, we can learn, we can make a training exercise, to focus our mind on all those positive and useful things. When we can do that, our experience will change, because there are also good things, positive things, not only negative things for us to focus on. This is a very important point that I repeatedly emphasise.

Maybe you already know this in theory – as I only know it also in theory - but I think all of us need to use this in practice. That is why I say it again and again. It is one thing to know it in theory, it is totally another thing to actually put it into practice. If we can really do that, it transforms our life - it really transforms our life. Then we can become less disturbed by things that usually disturb us and thereby find much more calm, peace and joy. We are much more okay with whatever happens, to us or around us. This is what we call peace of mind: when we don't get easily blown away with things happening, or emotions arising, problems occurring and so on.

Although everything that we do is intended to bring us more happiness, more satisfaction, more joy, more freedom from problems, getting that result does not depend on the problems alone, but is about the way we react to those problems. I think this is the most important thing.

I don't think I can emphasise it enough, because, 'all problems finished' is almost impossible. There will never be a time when all problems are finished, when there are no more problems happening to me and around me and all over the world. That can never happen. So the only possible way to deal with this is through learning how to react.

This does not mean that we should not try to solve problems. Of course we should solve problems also; if we can resolve a problem, that is very good for us, that is very good for others, that is good for everybody. But resolving a problem is also about ourselves, how we react to it. When you have the confidence born of knowing that whatever happens, you can be okay, when you can experience yourself in that way, then you have become a really stable practitioner.

That is what a true stable practitioner is. There are no special, strange experiences – feelings such as, "Oh, now I am enlightened" or, "I feel a very special kind of sensation here, I feel as if I am inseparable from everybody." Or, "I feel so joyful, I feel so compassionate." These, and many other kinds of experiences are temporary. It is a nice experience, but in the end it doesn't really count at all.

If you experience a little of the confidence described above, you will not have a totally different way of perceiving the world. It will still be the same as that of everybody else. If you feel, "I know how to deal with problems, I know how to experience myself in such a way that it is okay, that is not going to be only joyful and blissful." Your experience will not be all rainbows and flowers, you will not feel you are flying or floating in the air. It is not automatically like that. As the text says, it doesn't happen like this.

We need to train, step by step and we can begin with small things. How do I react when somebody says something that I don't like very much, for example: "You are really fat and old?" I can say, "Okay, I am fat and old, so what?" What is there to be afraid of or to be annoyed about? It could be nice - it is a reminder. Sometimes it is a good thing to remind yourself, because we all have lots of misunderstandings. You probably feel that you are really great, or that you will never ever die. You have this deluded thinking that you are able to stay the same way all the time. Here is a story I have told many times before:

A monk in a monastery in Tibet made friends with a certain kind of spirit. He was a very nice spirit so he brought food, drink and anything else the monk wanted. So the monk lived a very comfortable life. But since he knew that he has to practice Dharma in order to be able to die well, he told the spirit: "You are a spirit, so you know things a little bit better than me. Therefore when I am starting to approach my death, please let me know. Then I will start to practice Dharma."

So the spirit said, "Yes, I will do that, that's no problem."

Some time later he came and said, "Your hair has grown grey."

The monk replied, "You only see it now? I have had grey hair for a long time, that is nothing new."

The spirit said, "Oh, you already know about it?"

"Of course I know about it, I have grey hair."

The spirit thought, okay, and went away.

Then, after some time he came back again, and said, "You have lost your teeth, you have practically no teeth left now."

The monk said, "What are you talking about? I have been losing my teeth for many years now, I have almost no teeth."

"Oh, you know?"

"Of course I know."

"Okay, then that's very nice," said the spirit and went away.

Then, some time later he came back again and said to the monk, "I think you are going to die tomorrow."

"What!" said the monk, "But I told you to remind me, a long time ago, that when I am nearing death, you should tell me."

"But I told you many times," said the spirit. "I said your hair was going grey, and you said you knew about it. I said your teeth were falling out and you said you knew about it. So I thought you knew you were getting older and, so, nearing death."

So, when someone tells you, "You look really old," or anything like that, it is a good reminder. It is so great.

When you can take small things lightly, then I think you can slowly learn to take slightly bigger things well also. If you can make a habit of maintaining a little mindfulness, after some time it will become easy. We don't always have to feel that we need to protect ourselves. In fact, we don't have to defend ourselves all the time. Let people say things, let people criticise, let people give their opinions. That alone doesn't make our case defenceless. Sometimes it's easier if you let people say things. Because if it is not the truth, if to your way of thinking you have done nothing wrong, then you don't need to defend yourself. The defence is already there.

As soon as somebody says, "It feels as if you are being a little bit..." you defend yourself. That makes people attack you even more. It happens like that. Then we should slowly, step by step, try to change the way we experience our emotions, the way we react to other people, the way we react to problems and difficulties. And that is the practice. Actually, there is nothing else.

That is why I always say that I don't practise Buddhism. I just practise on myself. I think it is the same for many other people. I don't feel as if I am practising Buddhism. I am trying to work on myself – my own emotions, my own reactions, my own problems and habitual tendencies. And that is practising Dharma.

There are many teachings and instructions taught by the Buddha, and by great masters who were his followers, which I could use. I may not understand all of them, I may not be familiar with all of them, but I can understand some of them, and those I can use. But a very good instruction doesn't need to be necessarily from a religious or spiritual tradition. If anybody, or anything, from any field, in any subject, in any kind of culture, helps me or inspires me to work on myself, there is absolutely no reason why I shouldn't use that.

Patrul Rinpoche said, "Even if someone who is totally drunk and has a hundred different faults gives you good advice, you should take it." Why not? It is good that you take good advice. It's good to give advice also. Somebody said once, "You should give children advice. Of course, they will not listen to you, but they will pass it on to their children!" So, therefore, take advice; and give advice if you find something is helpful. And then, of course, if possible, use it yourself as well.

In the breaks between sessions, pray to your Lama and the Three Jewels that you may be able to use your suffering as your path.

That means that you also make prayers to ask for help and blessings from enlightened beings that you may develop the ability to succeed with this practice.

When your mind has grown slightly stronger, when you have some confidence that you can do this a little bit, then make offerings to the Three Jewels and to negative forces and insist: 'Please send me misfortune and obstacles, so I can work on developing the strength of my practice.' At the same time, always, always, stay confident and cheerful.

This is an important point, because if you want something, then it is not a problem anymore. If you are able to ask, "May there be some problems and obstacles, so that I can really work on them", and you really have the capacity to not mind having difficulties, or even want to have some, then you have definitely attained a level of stability.

When you first begin this training, it is vital to distance yourself from ordinary social activities. Otherwise, caught up in the business of everyday preoccupations, you will be influenced by all your misguided friends asking questions like: 'How can you bear to put up with so much suffering, so much humiliation?'

This is something it is possible to do in Tibet, but not here in the West. You cannot go into a retreat to do your training. But here you have something good, something like a retreat. It is called privacy. You go into your room and then nobody disturbs you. That is a special feature of the West, so you can do it at home. In Tibet, we never had that, there was nothing called privacy. Here, you have privacy, and that is your retreat. You can do things in the privacy of your own space.

Besides, endlessly worrying about enemies, relatives and possessions will cloud our awareness and upset our minds beyond all our control. So that means we will inevitably go astray and slide into bad habits. Then, on top of this we will be swept away by all kinds of distracting objects and situations.

So we have to be mindful and see that we don't get too influenced by others. Because people always give you suggestions. Most of the time they have good intentions. Yet sometimes the intention is not so good because they are under the influence of their own reactions, their own habitual tendencies, or way of being, which is based on ignorance. It is very difficult not be influenced in a very negative way by such things, based as they are on the usual samsaric way of reacting. When everybody reacts in a certain way, we tend to think that we should also react in the same way: this is very strong.

But in the solitude of retreat environments, since none of these are present, awareness is very lucid and clear and so it is easy to make your mind do whatever you want it to do.

It is still not easy, but maybe easier under such circumstances, I don't know.

It is for this reason that when practitioners of Chöd train in 'trampling right on top of suffering,' at the beginning, they put off doing the practice using the harm caused by human beings and amidst distraction, but instead, make a point of working with the apparitions of gods and demons in cemeteries and other desolate and powerful places.

Those who practise Chöd go to cemeteries or other frightening places such as those where ghosts are thought to be, to work on their own fear. This is both because we have to work on our own fear as the first step and it makes it easier to not have to have too many dealings with other people. Afterwards, when our own fears and other similar reactions are a little bit calmed, then we can try to work with other people and external situations. That is the Chöd way of training.

To sum up, not only so that your mind will be unaffected by misfortune and suffering, but also to be able to draw happiness and peace of mind out of these things themselves, what we need to do is this: Do not see inner problems like illness, or outer problems like rivals, spirits, or scandalous gossip, as something undesirable and unpleasant. Instead, simply get used to seeing them as something that you can work with, even as something pleasing and delightful. To accomplish this, we need to stop looking at harmful circumstances as problems. Make every effort to view them as beneficial. After all, whether a thing is pleasant or unpleasant comes down to how it is perceived by one's mind.

The right way of putting this is that we look at everything that happens as an opportunity to transcend and to transform. Then you will even be pleased to have a difficulty. Because we all like to have opportunities.

To take an example: someone who continually dwells on the futility of ordinary mundane occupations will only get more and more fed up as their wealth or circle increases. On the other hand, if someone sees worldly affairs as meaningful and beneficial they will seek, and even pray, to increase their power and influence.

With this kind of training then, our mind and character will become gentler and more peaceful. We will become more open and more flexible. We will be easier to get along with, we will be courageous and confident, we will be freed from obstacles that hinder our Dharma practice, we will be able to turn any negative circumstances to our advantage. We will meet with success, glory and auspiciousness will accompany us and our mind will always be content in the happiness born of inner peace.

If we can practise this teaching well, we should be able to get the above result.

To follow a spiritual path in this degenerate age, we cannot be without armour of this kind.

So, this is the most important practice. Meditation is important, but this is more important than meditation. This is something that you can do anywhere, everywhere, any time - not only in a Buddhist centre. That is why I say you do not need extra time to do Dharma practice.

It is not because we have no time that we don't practise Dharma. It is either because we don't know how to do it, or we don't have the discipline to do it. When we can practise in this way, we can work with any problem concerning our reactions, our emotions, our negative feelings such as sadness, anger or fear, any kind of loneliness, problematic situations and our reactions to other people. The practice of working with these things is not about time, it is about how we react.

If we can really practise in this way, then that is true practice. It is real practice because then there is something that we can really transform. It is much, much more than meditation. Meditation is also good. It is a way to try to calm your mind and learn how to be mindful and learn how to be relaxed in a natural way. Of course that is a practice too. But this is something that can really transform us, so therefore I sometimes feel it is a much more powerful practice than any kind of meditation.

> *Because if we are no longer tormented by the suffering of anxiety and irritation, not only will other kinds of suffering fade away like soldiers who have lost their weapons, but even misfortunes like illness will, as a rule, vanish on their own.*

Many side effects arise from our mind becoming peaceful; many other things may improve.

> *The saints of the past used to say, "If you are not unhappy or discontented about anything, then your mind will not be disturbed. Since your mind is not disturbed, the subtle wind energy will not be disturbed. That means the elements of your body will also not be disturbed. The result of all these not being disturbed, is the turning of the wheel of happiness."*

Not only will you have more joy, more peace and more stability in your mind, but your body will also be affected. Even small illnesses and other imbalances could be harmonised, if the practice is done properly.

Question: Abuse, hurt and letting go

Student: Talking about abuse and the victims of abuse: for many years it was not acceptable for people to talk about abuse, - I am thinking of abuse of all different kinds, including the atrocities that happen during wars. These things were suppressed and taboo, so victims could not talk about it. There are examples of when people could then talk about these things, ten or twenty years later, it felt for many as if the experience had just happened, it was still very fresh in people's memories. I think it was made especially bad because the victims couldn't talk about it. What do you think?

Rinpoche: Maybe it is that people don't want to accept that these things happen, or they want to deny that they happen to other people, and so it becomes taboo to talk about them. But if something has happened to me, it is not always necessary that I have to talk about it with others in order to make it better. Even if I do talk about it, the talking doesn't really change things; the talking is not the main point. The main point is how I react to what has happened to me.

Sometimes talking can help a little. If I express something, it becomes slightly lighter and I don't have to keep it in my mind all the time. That is true. But, basically, I think talking is not the solution - the solution lies in changing your way of looking at it.

When some very negative thing happens to me, I say to myself, "This is not such a nice thing, but it has happened. It happened but I don't have to feel too bad that I had to go through it. It was happening to me, it happened and then it finished. So, now I am very happy it has finished." When I have that way of looking, then whatever has happened does not give me continuous problems.

If I cannot allow myself to let go of what happened by saying, "This is the past, let it be," and instead I say, "That was something terrible, how can that have happened to me? Something dreadful has happened to me," and so on, then I think the effect will remain in my mind. I think the common social outlook then brings more harm. Because society's view of abuse is that it is so shocking, the abuse becomes a taboo and this makes it impossible for you to talk about what has happened to you. When society has so much aversion to these things, your way of looking easily becomes similar and you develop so much aversion that you cannot simply let it go. This outlook in society actually makes you hold onto the problem more.

We really need to work on these things and learn to transform them. We need to not only talk about them, but work on letting go from within. Many people who have gone through various kinds of abuse almost think that it is their fault and they develop feelings of guilt. Then their way of seeing things becomes really complicated.

I think that when we can develop a simpler way of looking at abuse, then it will be easier to transform how to respond to it. Of course, this is a difficult subject. It is a difficult thing to say, but I really find that some people who have gone through abuse hold on to it very tightly. Then if somebody says, "You should let it go," they become angry and say, "How can I let go of it? It is totally impossible!" It seems that they don't want to let it go, they are so identified with it.

I see this very clearly in many people, and it makes it impossible for them to let go. It is not only the fact of having gone through abuse, but somehow there is a whole process that comes together, involving all sorts of factors: the cultural background; the social background; your own way of looking at things. This creates such strong identification with the abuse that it becomes almost impossible to let go. The feeling 'this is me' has developed around it. So that if you say, 'let go' they become defensive; they turn on you and attack you. This means even the possibility of letting go cannot develop. And this is the more serious problem, I think.

Student: Is it important to become aware of, to become conscious about, what has actually happened?

Rinpoche: You mean in cases of abuse? I don't know. There are many things we don't want to face. We push them out of sight and then forget about them. There are some experiences that make an impression on us, but then we forget them and we have problems later because of that. There are countless numbers of instances like that (which also come from previous lifetimes); but this is another subject. What we are talking about here is mainly what we experience now.

We need to create a habit that, when something negative happens, we then face it and work with it. If we do that, then the habit of ignoring and neglecting such things, which means they get lodged in our unconscious store, can slowly change. This is the way to go forward.

Student: Can we take time over this?

Rinpoche: Yes, you can take as much time as you like. Because this is about life, it is not about time. Whether we remember it or we don't remember it, anything that has happened to us, anything at all, is something that it is no use to hold on to. We cannot actually hold on to any experience and there is no need to. So, therefore, I can start to train to let things be. To allow myself to be. And this is a way of being natural. You could say, "Dare to be! Dare to be yourself." That is the kind of attitude that we should train in and develop.

Student: As a victim of violence at the hand of someone who was quite close to me, I understand what you said before. But what I would like to ask is whether you think it is best to work on this by myself and stay away from the person who was violent? Or should I get in contact with this person and work it out together? Would it be better just to say no, I don't want to be in contact? I do not want to have bad feelings and say to the person, "No, you are bad and I don't want to talk with you anymore." But how can I find a way to forgive this person, to really forgive?

Rinpoche: If this person is repentant for what he or she has done and wants to work with you, that is a good thing, then you can work together. But generally we are not talking about other people, we are only talking about ourselves - what I can do, myself. Because it is difficult to control the actions of other people. The practice is not about involving other people. If other people co-operate and participate, then maybe there is no problem with that, and it could be very good. But that is another matter. Here, we are talking about what I can do, how can *I* change? Other people may not even want to acknowledge things that have happened, so their involvement is something over which we have no control. *What I can do*: this is something that we have control over.

We are not talking about what is right or wrong, or who is to be punished, or what course of action you should take. We are talking about how you can have fewer problems with what happened. That is the main thing. You have gone through difficult times, from your near ones, maybe from your dear ones, whoever it may be – far or near, it doesn't matter - but now, what can you do so that you have less problems in your life? That is the issue.

Of course you have to think, "That was a very bad thing that happened." But if you keep repeating, "It was a very bad thing, it was a very bad thing," it won't help you. It makes it even worse, because you are holding on to something negative and then it tortures you all the time.

It is much more important for you to focus on the thought, "That happened, this person behaved in such a way; that was very bad. But I do not need to hold on to that any more. It's something that happened to me, but it is finished and so now I don't want to hold onto that any more."

The other person will go through his or her own negative karma; they will have their own problems, maybe later on. That doesn't matter here. That is their own case, and has its own causes. So, if they repent and do their own purification, that is also good, but that is their business.

What you have to do now is to let go. Let go as much as possible, saying, "That happened. Now I am not going to hold on to it, I am going to let it go. I'm going to relate to it in a different way."

Forgiveness is not that you say, "Now this person is freed from all the problems that were created and I can like them now." It is not like that.

To think that all these things that happened have now kind of become good, that is not forgiveness. Forgiveness is the understanding that if I hold on to this negative feeling, it is not good for me. So therefore I refuse to be angry, I refuse to be hurt. I let go. I forgive.

The main problem in relation to past abuse is the hurt, isn't it? A hurt feeling is a cause of suffering which is very bad for me. Therefore, it is better for me if I do not hold on to this hurt feeling. Maybe it was someone near to me, maybe someone far from me, but whatever they did, they did it. They did something bad; but how much hurt I feel now is my choice, that is up to me.

Even if somebody is doing something really bad, really hurtful, to me, I can still refuse to be hurt. I can say, "I don't want, I will not, I refuse, to be hurt because that is not good for me. Maybe this person wants to hurt me, maybe this person doesn't want to hurt me – I don't know. But I refuse to be hurt, I don't want to hold on to any hurt feeling. I am okay now, more or less. I would like to be a better human being, I would like to enjoy the way I am now. I don't want to stay hurt, I don't need to keep this hurt feeling anymore. It's useless, it's bad for me, so therefore I don't want to hold on to it, I will not hold on to it. I will feel joyful about all the other good things in my life."

I do not allow my life to be ruined just because some silly person did some stupid thing to me. I am not allowing him or her to ruin my life just because something happened. To have that attitude is what is important.

Whether or not you ever talk to that person again, is a different topic. The important point is that you don't allow yourself to remain hurt by what happened. So therefore, you let it go. You transform it.

Student: I understand what you say, but I still ask myself how I should behave towards the people who hurt me in daily life. Should I stay away from them and say, "I don't want this at all?" Just how much should I tolerate and forgive?

Rinpoche: That is up to you. It is not that it has to be done this way or that way. It is up to you. But the main thing is that you don't allow yourself to be hurt. Because how much you allow yourself to be hurt is up to you, it is your decision. Once you are not feeling hurt, it is easier to decide the next step.

If you want to talk to that person, if you want to socialise with them or not, it is up to you. That depends on how you feel. You don't have to talk to them: why should you talk to them if they are hurting you? But, if you feel that it is good, it is okay, to talk to them, then talk to them. That is also okay. But, more important than that, is you, yourself.

I think that once you have really been able to make yourself feel, "I don't allow myself to feel hurt, I let go," then it is not so important anymore whether you see that person or not. If this person is around, it is okay - you never allow them to hurt you again. It is not that you judge him or her, or don't judge them. There is no question of approving, or not approving of what that person did, or absolving them from blame.

Forgiveness is not that. Forgiveness is that you don't want to hold on to the incident anymore, so you just take that feeling of hurt away and throw it into the wastepaper bin. That is extremely important. That person is not important for you, you are the one that is important for you.

There is also another way of looking at this, which can also help: you can understand that the harmful action somebody performed happened because they were under the power of their own negative emotions, and so on. When people are under the very strong influence of negative emotions they do many bad things. That is samsara, we have talked about this. People even harm themselves: many people harm themselves. But really nobody wants to harm themselves – everybody is afraid of being harmed. But, if people are overpowered by negative emotions, they do harm themselves; they even kill themselves sometimes.

So, therefore, if people harm others, it is not a big shock. It is more of a shock that they harm themselves. If you can understand it in this way, that they have done it because they are under the power of a very difficult, negative situation, you may not hate them, you can feel sorry for them. This is also a way of dealing with them. But the main thing is that you don't need to be hurt.

———

Back to the text:

> *Horses and donkeys with sores on their backs from carrying heavy loads are easy prey for scavenging birds. People who are prone to fear are easy victims to negative spirits, but not those whose character is stable and strong.*

When horses and donkeys who have been overworked develop open sores on their backs, birds and insects come and cause them even more pain. In the same way, people who have too much fear and sensitivity, too much aversion to unhappiness and suffering, become overly susceptible to those things, they are easily overcome by sufferings, pains and problems. To deal with this, it is very important that we try to develop stability. Here, 'stability' means that we learn to take small problems and unwanted occurrences in our stride. Instead of letting such things upset us, we can even see them as an opportunity to practise. If we can really do that, it becomes an important opportunity for us, because then we have a way to transform that suffering, a way to overcome it.

> *Thus, the wise, seeing that all happiness and suffering depend upon mind, will seek their happiness and well-being within their mind.*

Those who are wise understand that how unhappy or how happy they are, how much they suffer and how joyful they are, does not only depend on what is happening around them, or to them. It is not the circumstances that they find themselves in, but how they respond to them, which makes the difference. Their happiness depends mainly on their state of mind and how they respond to their life. If they have that understanding, they can also know that their well-being and happiness are more dependent on their response to a situation than on that situation itself.

> *Since all the causes of happiness are entirely within themselves, they will not be dependent on anything external. Which means that nothing whatsoever, be it sentient beings or anything else, can do them harm.*

It is not that I cannot be harmed – there are many ways in which people can harm me: they can take things away from me, they can create obstacles for me and so on. But nobody can take away my own peace of mind, if I am the master of it. And they cannot even take away my own confidence and my own understanding of how to respond to situations, if I have learned how to work with this in a very clear and strong way. Then, my confidence, my joy, my happiness, my peace of mind cannot be taken away nor can they be crushed by anybody or anything.

> *Even when they die, this attitude will follow them so they will always, always be free and in control.*

If we can learn this way of being and develop it, then that can carry us even through our death. Even when death comes, we will know that there is nothing to fear, that fear is no use and what we have to go through, we have to go through. So we will take it as a challenge, as an opportunity. We will take any kind of experience that comes in a positive spirit.

When that kind of experience or understanding comes, then you really become free. Freedom does come partly from outside, but true freedom can only be found within yourself. If you can free yourselves from your fear, if you can free yourselves from being limited to following sensations and emotions, and instead know that you can be okay and you can face and deal with any experience you have, then you are really free.

That freedom is true peace of mind.

When that kind of freedom and peace of mind comes, then you are totally, completely and genuinely free. Because then nobody controls you. Whatever happens, nothing can totally overwhelm you. This is, therefore, the main objective of the practice of Dharma - transforming our suffering, transforming our happiness. This means that our happiness will then not depend on outer circumstances or people, and our suffering or pain or unhappiness will also not depend on circumstances or other people. It depends on how we react, and when we know that this is the case, then we are free.

This is just how the bodhisattvas attain their meditative stabilisation, the samadhi, called 'bliss pervading all experiences.'

In Buddhist terminology, this is called 'the samadhi in which everything is blissful.' 'Samadhi' means meditative stabilisation, so anybody who can experience this, can learn this, can master this, has the attainment that their mind is always stable and in peace, and therefore in bliss.

'Bliss' here is not like a state of excitement; it means that your mind is never overwhelmed. It is free and therefore happy, joyful and light in whatever circumstances you find yourself. When the translation says, 'bliss pervading all experiences,' what it means to say is that all experiences are overwhelmed, or controlled, or influenced, by our blissful state of mind.

Unwise people chase after external objects and experiences in the hope of finding happiness.

Most of us think that it is external objects that give us happiness, so we chase after them. We think that if we have a big house, a good job, good friends and so on, that will give us happiness. It is not that they are bad or they are not needed, but these things are not a stable basis for happiness because they always change. What we can get, we can also lose, and therefore we cannot really rely on them. If we do, we are always either in the process of trying to find those things or in fear of losing them. If we think that our happiness can depend on such things, we are wrong.

Finally, your happiness doesn't depend on them in any case, because if you have the wrong attitude, you can even have everything that you want and still be unhappy. If the way you are, the way you respond to things, is not okay, you can always be unhappy. Even if you think you have everything, you will always have the fear of losing those things, the urge to protect them and the wish to try to get even more. It is never the case that you are really completely satisfied and at peace.

> *But whatever happiness they do find, great or small, it always turns out like the saying:*

> *You're not in control; it's all in others' hands.*
> *As if your hair were caught up in the branches of a tree.*

Suppose you have long hair and are taking a walk in the woods, and your hair gets tangled in a thorny bush. Then what kind of a situation are you in? Your hair is tangled and holds you back. You are unable to move. You are caught and can't walk away. You cannot sit; and you cannot let be either. Actually, you find yourself in a very difficult predicament. Giving away all your freedom to others is exactly like that.

As long as we think that our circumstances depend upon outer things, then we will never be free because we so strongly rely upon other things, in both small and big ways. We become like slaves, dependent upon other people and things. As a result, they control us and we are not free.

When you constantly assume that your happiness depends upon someone else, then the saying goes that nothing good will happen; you constantly have problems or have to put up with unfulfilled wishes. If you think that your happiness is totally dependent on external things, like having a good house, it is always going to be a struggle.

However, happiness can depend, not on other things, but on yourself. If you know you can be happy just to be in a room, with enough space around you so that you can lie down, or in a small tent, a palace, a slum, or anywhere else, that means you are happy. And your happiness is not dependent on what kind of house you live in, or what kind of people you live with. It doesn't mean that better is not better, but it means you become free and you are not totally dependent. It is no longer like your hair is caught up in the tree.

What you hope for never comes to be, things never come together, or else you make misjudgments and there is only one failure after another.

If you feel that your happiness is totally dependent on other people, or on what is happening around you, then your situation becomes like this: something is okay, but something else is not okay; something comes and something else doesn't come. Then you misjudge and one thing is okay but another fails. Then, when it is like that, you always have to run after something and run away from something else.

And enemies and thieves have no trouble harming you. Even the slightest false accusation can separate you from your happiness.

When it is like that, you can be harmed by anything, by anybody, in every circumstance. A small accusation, that someone is not very happy with you, someone not liking you so much or looking at you in a not so accepting way – that can make you completely unhappy. This means that you are dependent on them. If you need to be liked by everybody, to be accepted and loved by everybody, then you are too much reliant on external things. And they never go okay. It is like that.

However much a crow looks after a baby cuckoo, it can never turn it into a baby crow.

It is said that a cuckoo lays its egg in a crow's nest, and when it hatches, the cuckoo chick is a little bigger than those of the crow, so it throws them out of the nest. Then it's the only one remaining so it can grow very quickly from the mother crow feeding it. But the cuckoo cannot become a crow. And in the same way, if you believe your happiness is dependent on other people, other things, other circumstances, then it's not possible to have real stability and peace of mind. Because you are not free, you always have to rely on somebody else or something else.

In the same way, if all your efforts are misguided, and based on something unreliable, there will be nothing but fatigue for the gods, negative emotions for the spirits, and suffering for yourself.

Relying for happiness on external factors never comes to anything really stable or useful. It will always bring fatigue, it will always bring negative emotions, and it will always bring pain and problems for us. So we need to learn how to be independent, how to be okay whatever happens to us.

If I am alone I should be happy, I should make the best of it. I can think: "It's so nice to be alone, because I am free, I am not compelled to do anything. If I want to go out, I can go out, if I want to stay in, I can stay in, if I want to sleep all day, I can sleep all day. I don't need to rely on anybody or depend on anything; I can meditate all day if I want."

If I am together with other people, then there is another way. I can enjoy being together with others and that is also okay. It's not the circumstance that make us happy or unhappy, but how we are able to work with any kind of situation as being okay for us – that is the secret of lifelong happiness. If we can learn that, then we have learnt how to transform, to transform both good things and bad things. So this is why the title of the text refers to both suffering and happiness.

This heart advice brings a hundred different essential instructions together into one crucial point.

This is the crucial advice for understanding how to find peace in yourself. Of all the many different methods, the different meditations, the different practices, this is the real essence. All the other practices lead to this experience, that you learn how to be okay in any circumstance, in every circumstance, and that you take anything happening – good or bad – as a challenge, as a practice, as something that you can accept and learn how to deal with, and even to like and enjoy.

When we can do this, we have really learnt how to transcend everything that can happen. So this is the understanding to cultivate.

There are many other pith instructions on accepting suffering and hardship in order to practise the path, and on transforming illness and destructive forces into the path, as taught, for example, in the pacifying tradition.

This is the Zhijey lineage of teaching founded by Padampa Sangye, and taught to Machig Labdrön [see *Chöd*] and many others. It is one of the eight practice lineages of Tibet.

But here, in a way, that is easy to understand, I have given a general outline of how to accept suffering, based on the writings of the noble Shantideva and his wise and learned followers.

All of this teaching on how to transform happiness and unhappiness is the essential message of Shantideva's *Bodhicharyavatara*, a text which is thoroughly and repeatedly studied by all students of Mahayana Buddhism. So this is the heart essence of the teachings coming from Shantideva and his followers.

This completes the teaching on how to transform our unhappiness and suffering from the point of view of the level of *kun dzob*, [Tibetan; 'deceptive appearances'], which is generally translated as 'relative truth'.

II - Relating to How Things Really Are

How to use the experience of suffering as a path to Enlightenment through the truth relating to how appearances really are.

The second section of the first part of the text concerns how to work in the context of absolute truth. Generally in Buddhism, reality as it appears is called 'relative reality;' reality as it actually is, is called the 'absolute truth.' Through an understanding of the latter, we can also transform suffering and happiness, but this is not explained in detail in our text, which continues:

By means of reasonings such as 'the refutation of production from the four extremes,' one's mind is drawn towards emptiness, the nature and condition of things, the supreme state of peace. And there is rest in this state, let alone harmful circumstances or suffering, not even their name can be found.

Sometimes we talk about emptiness, which is the true nature of mind or about the philosophy of *shunyata* [see *Emptiness*]. If we could really understand this, or realise this, then we would find that there is no need to run after or run away from things. There is nothing in me that can be really harmed, or can be really crushed or finished or anything like that. What I am is something interdependently arising, like an illusion, like a dream. It is not something that really exists, separately and independently. If we can have that understanding of how we are and therefore how everything else is, then there is no [need for?] fear and there is no need for anything else. There is no need to have any suffering, or problems, or pain. So that is a very strong and ultimate way of transforming any kind of problems or pain or suffering and thereby finding peace within ourselves.

This interdependently arising and empty quality is what Buddhist teachings refer to as the true, or absolute nature of things. According to these teachings it is very important to understand the true nature of things, to understand the absolute nature of yourself and all phenomena. This is not easy, it takes lots of time to study; there are many books, big treatises about this subject. However, intellectual understanding is not enough. We need to understand it practically and experientially. It is a big subject, therefore Do Drupchen Rinpoche did not write about it in detail here. He just made the point that we should slowly develop our understanding of it as much as we are able.

When the nature of everything is interdependent and empty, and that is the nature of my mind or myself also, then there is nothing fixed to depend on anything. Because of this, I am totally free. Even suffering is an interdependent thing, a totally fleeting thing. And all my emotions are also like that.

Then, what is there? There is nothing to hold on to. There is nothing that I need to grasp at. Every thought, every emotion, every experience is fleeting. They come, they go, they don't come from anything special and they don't go anywhere either. They are just momentary. What I am is also like that: arising and dissolving, that is what I am. There is nothing to find that exists totally in itself, and so there is nothing that can be destroyed either.

Once I really understand this nature that I have, I can be freed from any kind of fear. To understand this deeply, experientially, is to understand the absolute truth. When we completely understand the absolute truth, the truth of how things really are, then it becomes very clear how to react to the relative truth, the truth relating to what appears, or what happens. Everything is there and there is nothing we need to fear, there is nothing we need to run away from, there is nothing we need to run after, so therefore our mind becomes completely peaceful in a deep, a final way.

This is something very important, but it is not easy to realise. We have a very strong tendency to concretise, to see everything as solid and independently existing. We feel a very strong sense of being an individual, with everything else out there, concretely existing on its own. So therefore it is not easy for us to understand this; it needs much reflection, it needs some study so that we can deepen our understanding. This is why the text doesn't say much on this point. If you want to study, then you can go into it later.

Now we are talking about meditation. From a Buddhist point of view, everything that we experience is understood as included in the experience of our mind. Any experience or sensation, whatever is experienced – whether it is bodily sensations or thoughts - has to be experienced by mind. Otherwise it is not an experience.

The main purpose of meditation is to learn how to be undisturbed, how to experience everything without being disturbed, or how to be natural without being distracted by all sorts of problems – that is meditation. When we talk about bringing our mind under control, or making our mind flexible or calming our mind down; What these expressions are all trying to say is that we can just be at peace, whatever may happen. We do not need to be carried away by thoughts, emotions, sensations, problems and so on all the time. Meditation is a training for that. Generally our mind, as we all know, is very wild. One moment it is here, then another moment it's there. All sorts of thoughts, and all sorts of emotions run through it, and we are reacting all the time. Running after, running away – all the time.

Meditation in three steps

I like to describe meditation in three steps. The first is called 'bringing your body onto the seat.' This does not mean literally sitting. Sitting is one way you can meditate, but you can meditate while walking, while lying down, while eating, while doing anything at all. 'Bring your body onto the seat' means that you let go of all other activities, you disengage from everything that is going on around you. Because if you do not do this, your mind cannot be stable. From the moment that you start meditating, you just let everything rest. You bring your body to your seat, or to wherever you may be and you let things be. So that's the first step: bringing your body to the seat.

Bringing your mind into your body is the second, and this is very, very important. Our mind is always active and thinking. It thinks about everything, about all sorts of things happening. And it is almost always either in the past or in the future. Things happened in the past, things will happen in the future and all our stress, all our emotional problems have to do either with the past or the future. Something happened and we think, 'that was not good', or 'that was good.' Something might happen sometime in the future – 'that will be good, that won't be good,' like this. So all our fear and all our worries are always about the past or the future. When our mind is not here, but either in the past, whether yesterday or just the previous moment, or in the future, then it cannot settle.

When I say 'bring your mind into your body', it means now, at this moment. When your mind becomes one with your body, that means you are here, now: your mind is here now. In this body you see through your eyes, you hear through your ears. You feel with your body - only now, not yesterday, and not in the last moment. You see what is here now, you don't see what you saw yesterday or this morning. You hear what you hear just now, then another moment happens and that also is just now. So when we say 'bring your mind into your body,' it means you are here at this very moment, totally together and aware of everything that is happening around you. That brings your mind into now.

And it is not that you have to be conscious of this. You don't have to be totally concentrated on anything. This is an important point; because when you concentrate, it becomes the past. "Oh, I see, yes, I saw this, I saw that." "I hear, yes I heard now, that was a bird, or what? Which kind of bird was it?" That is the past, that is thinking; then you are distracted.

If I can be just now in this very moment - what I see is what I see, what I hear is what I hear at this very moment, then this is now, and this is now, and this is now. So I see *now* but I see *now*, I hear now but I hear now. When I can be in this very present moment continuously, moment by moment, I am truly in presence – I am present. When I am in the present moment, then I am not in the past or future, and then I am not worrying about the future or reacting to the baggage of the past. I am just clear, direct and present, now.

When I can do that, when that is the way I am, I am in my nature. Because I am not speculating, I am just experiencing. Directly experiencing myself at this moment. And then I don't need to have stress, because I am not thinking.

Thinking, and being present, are two different things – thinking is about the past or future. Present awareness is what is here and now. So when we can be present now, at this very moment in this way, then we can be aware. Not thinking about the past or future but just aware now, moment by moment. When you can do that, you are free, your mind is free, your mind is at peace. There is no stress, because it is moment by moment. There is nothing to hold onto, there is no grasping – you cannot grasp, because the moment you grasp, the present is gone, it has become the past. This is how to meditate. We are not making a concept, we are just being. So this meditation is a technique for learning how to be in your natural way of being, with your mind and body together and your experience being that of the present moment, and not holding onto anything.

Not running after anything, not running away from anything. Then you are not struggling. If you are not running after anything, then you are not grasping. "I want this, I want that." You are not caught up in that, and you also have no fear because you are not running away from anything. And when you can really do that it is naturally peaceful. Because you dare to be the way it is. The more you realise that you can be in that state, the more joyful you are, because you have no story to follow, nothing to fear, nothing to run away from, nothing to run after – desire, attachment, grasping. So therefore, the more we can do that, the more serenity, the more peace we experience and therefore the natural joy of our mind can come up. And then there is peace. When you can really do that, then you will know what you are and what your mind is.

Because that *is* who you are, it is not a concept, it is not a philosophy, it is a direct experience of yourself. And the more you learn how to do that, the more you can deal with the present. If you can deal with the present moment, if you can be okay now, you can be okay in the next 'now', and the next – so you can be okay all the time. This is the meditation.

And so there are not too many concepts. Not too many because, in a way, there's not much to understand. Because all understandings are conceptual. However good they are, they are just concepts, philosophy. And they lie to you. So, if it is a thought, it doesn't count too much in experience. But meditation is not a thought, meditation is not a concept, meditation is learning to be in an experiential way, now.

The third point, after bringing your body to your seat and bringing your mind into your body, is 'bringing ease into your mind.' This means that you feel your mind to be at ease, kind of spacious, easy and relaxed. It means that you are just being. The only problem is that we are so used to being distracted - always now this thought, now that thought, our mind going everywhere. So, if that happens, if we are too busy, if we cannot simply be, then maybe we can rely a little on a technique, such as awareness using an object.

This can be your breathing – because this is something that you have to do whether you like it or not. Since you have to breathe in and breathe out, you can bring a gentle awareness to your breathing in. This does not mean a real concentration, just slight awareness, just to be in the present moment. Then when you are breathing out, be aware of breathing out. Slightly, just to be in the present moment. So that's how to start the meditation.

Sometimes people think, "When I meditate, I should have no thoughts, there should be nothing, just calmness." It's not like that: if thoughts come, no problem. But do not follow them. Just come down to your 'this moment'. If there are emotions that's okay. But not to follow them. Just be here and bring your mind back again and again to this very moment. And then relax. It's not about doing something, it's about not doing anything. It's just being. So therefore, being and being aware of being. That's it. Too much talking is not good.

Question: What to do?

Student: How can I overcome the sadness, or desperation, of belonging to a species, most of whom are so stupid and closed to understanding what life is all about? Everyone seems so focused on their own interests, they harm others and spoil the planet and are not able to think in the long term, just holding on to all this attachment and all the other problems we have been talking about. Even if I just talk about myself, it makes me so sad that it is hard to live with it.

Rinpoche: What can you do?

Student: Can you tell me?

Rinpoche: That's the thing. That's why we have been talking about this. It is not that I can do something about it right now. What I can do is first learn how to change a little bit so that I am not like that myself. It's no use only thinking about how stupid people are and then making myself more stupid by becoming angry and sad about it. It's of no use. So what I have to do is see that this is not the way to act. I can be concerned about all this, I can see the suffering, see the problem, and see that something needs to be done, but I cannot find something to do to change it all just like that. I need to work with myself. I have to start with myself. Being too much affected, too sad, or too angry doesn't bring any good to me, or to anybody else. So, therefore, the first thing is to try to let things be a little.

You have to let it be, because there is nothing you can do about it right now. You have to let be, so learn how to let be. If you can learn how to let be in yourself, at least you have become free from this tension of being too sad, or too angry. Then you can find a little bit of peace, in that you are accepting the situation as it has to be. There is no other way, you have to let it be okay. Even if you were to become so sad that you became mad, it wouldn't change the situation. It simply does no good.

But this doesn't mean that you should not do anything. We have to work on things patiently, step by step. That means, we have to understand what is going on, we have to understand everybody who is acting this way. They cannot help it, so there is no need to be angry. We have to be compassionate, we have to be understanding, and we have to have the understanding: "It is like that, maybe one day I will also be able to transform this in everybody, but first I need to transform it in myself."

So, bring patience, bring some diligence and inspiration for yourself to learn how to be, and how to respond. And try to transform in that way. The more you transform, the more you will create the capacity or the knowledge to help others. If you are drowning yourself, you cannot save somebody else. You have to learn how to swim if you want to save somebody from drowning. So that's why you have to first learn for yourself.

Student: I understand what you say, it is just that I wonder how these things can happen. If we go back to ancient times, the people were very poor, but closer to nature and better to each other. But now there is what we call civilization, which seems to have brought so much arrogance. I just don't understand how such stupidity can be repeated over and over like this.

Rinpoche: Well, we pride ourselves on being civilized and we say civilization should be much better than before. Maybe it is better in some ways, maybe it's worse in some other ways; but this expectation is none other than that: an expectation. It is also not the case that the old times were free of problems – there have been lots of problems. There are always problems.

Throughout history there have always been wars, fighting, atrocities and all sorts of violence. You can see from history that there has never been a time when everything was completely okay. That is how it is. We now have more weapons, more capacity to destroy. That is there, but we also have lots of other good things. But it is true that what civilization has brought is not only good things. So we need to develop, emotionally and intelligently. We need to develop our wisdom as well as our knowledge. Our knowledge of technology has advanced a lot. But our emotional maturity and our wisdom may not have developed at the same pace, and that is the problem.

Maybe we will develop, who knows? We have the capacity, if we want to. Human beings have the capacity to be compassionate, to be wise, to know what is good for ourselves and others. We do have the capacity for that. How much we use that capacity to develop as a society, as a race of human beings together, depends on what we do now. It depends on how much we value compassion, how much we value respect for each other, how much we value helping others, how much we think about the welfare of everybody else as a whole, as against thinking of 'my own.' I think that is where the balance point is.

If we have started to develop thoughts like, "I am what is most important. My interests are the most important thing. If lots of people get damaged in order for me to accomplish my desires and interests, then that is okay for me," then it will always create problems.

We don't have a sense of 'what is good for everybody is good for me too' - that is what we need to develop. There is an ancient Sanskrit saying:

"For the sake of the world, I sacrifice my country.
For the sake of the country, I sacrifice my village.
For the sake of the village, I sacrifice my family.
For the sake of my family, I sacrifice myself."

If we could have that attitude, then I think everything would become okay. Because if the world goes bad, then your country cannot be good. If your country goes bad, then your village cannot be the only good village. And if your village goes bad, your family cannot be good in isolation from that. You cannot be the only survivor in the whole universe.

Sometimes this whole way of thinking is reversed these days. Now it is even sometimes said in reverse: "For the sake of my country I sacrifice the world, for the sake of my village, I sacrifice my country, for the sake of my family I sacrifice everything else, for the sake of me, I sacrifice everybody, including my family." That mentality is contrary, it is the opposite of what we call compassion. This is the only problem. If this can change this, the world can become a very good place very quickly; we have the capacity.

Some scientists say that we are already a little bit too late to prevent the climatic disaster. But that is only bad for human beings. The world will survive; human beings may or may not survive.

Taking Joy as the Path

How to use the experience of happiness as a path to enlightenment

The second part of the main text contains two parts: how to use the experience of happiness from the perspective of relative truth [the truth relating to the world of appearances or how things commonly appear to us] and how to use it in relation to the absolute dimension [of how things are in reality].

I - At the Level of Relative Appearances

First, how to use the experience of happiness at the level of relative appearances.

Whenever happiness and its various causes appear, if we slip under their power, then we will grow increasingly conceited, smug and lazy, which will block our spiritual path and progress. In fact, it is difficult not to be carried away by happiness, as Padampa Sangye pointed out:

"We human beings can cope with a lot of suffering, but very little happiness."

That is why we need to open our eyes in whatever way we can to the fact that happiness and the things that cause happiness are all actually impermanent and by nature suffering. So try your best to arouse a deep sense of disillusionment and to stop your mind indulging in its usual apathy and negligence. Say to yourself, 'Look: all the happiness and material wealth of this world is trivial and insignificant and brings with it all kinds of problems and difficulties too.

Still, in a certain sense, it does have its good side: Buddha said someone whose freedom is impaired by suffering will have great difficulty attaining enlightenment, but for someone who is happy, it is easier to attain.

What good fortune then, to be able to practice the Dharma in a state of happiness like this. So from now on, in whatever way I can, I must convert this happiness into Dharma, and then, from the Dharma, happiness and well-being will continuously arise. That is how I can train in making Dharma and happiness support one another. Otherwise I always end up where I started, like someone trying to boil water in a wooden saucepan.'

The main point to get here is that whatever happiness, whatever well-being, comes our way, we must unite it with the practice. This is the whole vision behind Nagarjuna's 'Garland of Jewels'.

Even though we may be happy, if we don't recognise it we will never be able to make use of that happiness as an opportunity for practicing the Dharma. Instead, we will be forever hoping that some extra happiness will come our way, and we will waste our lives on countless projects and actions. The antidote to this is to apply the practice wherever it is appropriate. And above all, to savour the nectar of contentment.

There are other ways of turning happiness into the path, especially those based on recalling the kindness of the Buddha, Dharma and Sangha, and on the instructions for training in Bodhicitta, but this will do for now. As with using suffering as a path, so with happiness too. You need to go to a solitary retreat environment and combine this with practice of purification and accumulating merit and wisdom.

Sometimes this translation says 'transforming suffering and happiness,' sometimes it says, 'using happiness, or suffering, as the path to enlightenment.' But the main thing that we should understand from the text at this point is that happiness and unhappiness are like two sides of the same coin. It is the same with aversion and attachment: the more attachment you have, the more aversion will arise also. If I like something too much, that will create a lot of fear of not getting it, or of getting its opposite. In the same way, if I have too much aversion to unhappiness, then I want to have happiness too much. Too much wanting happiness brings me lots of unhappiness - because I might not get it, and if I get a little bit, I need more, and so on. It is very important to understand this relationship.

When some good things happen in our life, we tend to take them for granted, we let them go to our heads. Then we get many problems and everything goes wrong. It is very good when everything goes well, or when some things are going well. We should recognise that, we need to appreciate that. But we also need to understand that everything changes. It will all change and nothing is really permanent; everything is passing. Therefore we should make the best of it, but not be too attached to it.

If something good happens, that is very nice and we should make the best of it but if we get too much attached to it – "Oh, it's so good!" – then, immediately we have the worry of losing it and the worry of what will happen then. And then when it does go, it's very shocking and problematic for us. It brings us a lot of pain and problems. We need to understand this and see it for what it is.

When things go right, it is very good, we should be happy, we should appreciate things. But it is also okay even if it does not happen like this, even if it all goes wrong. To have that understanding, that confidence, that way of being, is very important. Because without that, then some success, some happiness, some good things happening for us, will not bring a stable happiness. They will only bring more worries and more problems.

Therefore, when you think, "When happiness is there, everything goes well," you should look at it as impermanent and as having the nature of suffering. This is not to say that happiness is bad. It is just that we have to look at this happiness, we have to accept it in a proper way and then it will be very good and useful. If we take it in a wrong way, if we grasp at it, then not only does it not last, but this grasping will also bring many problems. We need to understand this. And in order to do so, we have to think about disillusionment and what it is associated with.

Of course, when good things happen that is very good and we should take them as an opportunity. And as we have said before, we should also take even problems, or suffering, pain and unhappiness as an opportunity. So of course we should take good things such as success and happiness as an opportunity, even more so. We should appreciate them and use them in the best possible way. Sometimes we are able to do this. But sometimes good things happen in our life and we take them for granted and we don't appreciate them.

If we are healthy, we say: "So what? Yes, I am healthy." Only when we become sick, do we say, "Ah, it was so nice when I was healthy, it was so nice when I didn't have a headache." Sometimes we have a headache and we say "Ooh, this headache is the worst thing, if I can get rid of this headache, then I won't mind if I have a pain in my knees." But then, when we have a pain in the knees, we say, "Pain in the knees is the worst." It is like that.

When we do that, when we take good things for granted, then we make a big deal about even a small problem or a little thing not going right. "I am healthy, I'm okay, everything going well, my life is okay but that is nothing. Germany didn't win the football and that is a problem. I feel like complaining to the German football association. Or the coach." Sometimes people say things like that.

We need to clearly understand that when we have good things, we should appreciate them. Then, when other things are not going right, it is the moment to understand that that is also okay. Of course this does not mean that we should do nothing about those difficulties.

The text says very clearly that we need to use these practices in our life. The practice of Buddhism is absolutely nothing else other than this, and this is very important to understand. Some people ask, "Can I practise Dharma even if I don't want to do any meditation, or pujas, or go into any temples? Or if I just do those things a little bit?" When you go through this kind of teaching, which is the most essential, the most authentic, the heart-essence of the Buddhist practice, you find there is nothing mentioned about pujas, there is nothing mentioned about meditation or anything else. It is all about how we take life.

This is the practice. You can practise pujas, you can also not practise them. Meditation can be practised, or can be not practised. It depends on you. If you do the practice of this text, this is certainly the Buddha's practice. And nothing else is needed. This needs to be very clearly understood by anyone who is studying Buddhism. When the text says 'practice,' or 'integrate in your practice,' or 'make it a practice,' this does not mean that you find something to do, so that you mix it with some Buddhist rituals, for example. That is not what it is saying.

What it is saying is that you use whatever might be happening to you right now. Sometimes, when you are very unhappy, you think, "I cannot do any Dharma practice because I am too unhappy. I cannot do it because my problems are too great. I am too sad, too emotional, and so I can't practise." But then when you are happy, you also have no time to practise, because you are distracted.

Then your happiness becomes a problem. Because this practice is not for your leisure time. It is not an entertainment programme. It is for learning how to work with your own life, to make it better. If we don't use it when we need it, it is useless. It is like me, carrying bags full of medicines, but not taking any of them when I am sick.

So if the text says, 'use this teaching, practise it,' try to understand, try to become a little more mindful and clear. Develop that way of seeing and make yourself understand things properly, as it is described here.

If many problems arise for you, do not let that go too much to your head and say, "I have such problems, I am nothing, I am useless, I am finished." Or if you are a little bit successful, don't start to think, "I am so great" and become proud of yourself. Neither of these are necessary. If there are problems happening, remember they are not happening only for you, everybody has problems and not everything can be okay all the time.

We have to take the difficulties of our daily life as a challenge, as a path, as something to deal with. We have to do that. And if everything goes well, we also have to take that in the same way. We have to take things in the right way, so we can bring a certain stability to ourselves and learn how to deal with all the different situations of life. If we do that, then we are practising. This understanding is crucial. This is what has to be done.

It is your own practice so therefore you have to use your own understanding, your own experience, your own judgement and it's not something that can be spoon-fed: "At this moment you breathe in and hold it for a while. Then breathe out and hold your breath like that; yes, count one, two, three, and then breathe in again." It doesn't work like that. We are talking about a way of being that we need to learn from experience and then use in our own lives and slowly see how it works. This is an understanding, an attitude, a way of thinking rationally about our situation and our life. It is not only instruction, it is a guideline to be understood and then used in your own way. This is the practice.

II - In the Context of the Absolute Truth

Second, how to use the experience of happiness in the context of the absolute truth.

This section of the text deals with working on joy and happiness through the absolute truth. It is exactly the same procedure as working on suffering and pain: we let our minds be, through understanding the nature of things, through analysing, through meditating. When we can let our minds rest and be in a relaxed and peaceful state, when we can let things be, then our mind becomes peaceful and happy. Actually, we don't need to do too much in order to be happy. If we can really let our minds be, letting our minds be natural and relaxed, then peace and happiness arise naturally. It is only difficult because we are not used to it.

Sometimes we do not want to change things simply because we are too engrossed in what is going on. We have so much fear and so many doubts, that it becomes not only difficult, but almost impossible, for us to change anything. But if we can really let ourselves and things be, if we really dare to relax, then ...

We can come to understand the nature of our mind, and the nature of everything else. This makes you dispassionate, through being able to see things very clearly. Then you understand that the whole point is not to get overwhelmed by any kind of experience; either with too much positive excitement, or with too much unhappiness and negative excitement, overwhelming you with shock and problems. When you understand the way things are, you can't fall back into the other way of being, because you are okay whatever happens. Nothing is a big deal because you know, basically, how things are.

It is often the case that we don't dare to do much, if anything at all; we don't dare to enjoy our lives, we don't dare to help others; we don't dare to rest and relax. We prefer being tense and nervous. Then there is more and more fear, more and more aversion; there are more and more quarrels and strife. But that is terrible! We should not be like that.

The more we understand the nature of things, then the more we realise that what I just described is not necessary at all, it's uncalled for, it's useless, because there is no reason to feel so insecure. Actually, there is no reason to feel insecure because there is no such thing as what is usually described as 'security.' Nobody can secure anything. Everything changes all the time, and all of us will die one day; nobody on this planet Earth can stop anybody from dying. So, why make such a big fuss about something like security, which is not at our disposal anyway?

When we understand this deeply, then we become more accepting - and more courageous. Courage comes from knowing that there is nothing to lose. John Wayne was always so brave in cowboy movies because he could say, "I have nothing to lose." It is true. When you have nothing to lose, you are brave. So, like that, when you deeply know that there is really nothing to lose, there is nothing to secure, then everything is okay. You then experience sincere relief.

Conclusion

What the training brings:

If we cannot practise when we're suffering because of all the anxiety we go through, and we cannot practise when we're happy because of our attachment to happiness, then that rules out any chance of our practising Dharma at all. That is why there is nothing more crucial for a practitioner than this training in turning happiness and suffering into the path.

If you do have this training, no matter where you live, in a solitary place or in the middle of a city; whatever the people around you are like, good or bad; whether you're rich or poor, happy or distressed; whatever you have to listen to, praise or condemnation, good words or bad; you'll never feel the slightest fear that it could bring you down in any way. No wonder this training is called the 'Lion-Like Yoga'.

Whatever you do, your mind will be happy, peaceful, spacious and relaxed. Your whole attitude will be pure, and everything will turn out excellently. Your body might be living in this impure world of ours, but your mind will experience the splendour of an unimaginable bliss, like the Bodhisattvas in their pure realms.

It will be just as the precious Kadampa masters used to say:

> Keep happiness under control;
> Put an end to suffering.
> With happiness under control
> And suffering brought to an end:
> When you're all alone,
> This training will be your true friend;
> When you are sick,
> It will be your nurse.

Goldsmiths first separate the impurities from gold by heating it, and then make it malleable by repeatedly quenching it. It is just the same with mind. If by working with happiness as your path, you become weary of it and disgusted with it, and by taking suffering as your path, you make your mind clear and cheerful, then you will easily attain the extraordinary samadhi which makes mind and body relaxed and capable.

This instruction, I feel, is the most profound of all, for it perfects discipline, the source of everything positive and wholesome. This is because not being attached to happiness creates the basis of the extraordinary discipline of renunciation, and not being afraid of suffering makes this discipline completely pure.

According to the teaching:

> Generosity forms the basis for discipline;
> And patience is what purifies it.

By training in this practice now, when you attain the higher stages of the path, this is what it will be like:

> You will realise that all phenomena are like an illusion,

To be born again is just like walking into a lovely garden.
Whether you face prosperity or ruin,
You'll have no fear of negative emotions or suffering.

Here are some illustrations from the life of the Buddha. Before
he attained enlightenment, he abandoned the kingdom of
a universal monarch as if casting away a straw and lived by
the River Narainjana, without a care for the harshness of the
austerities he was practising. What he showed was that in order to
accomplish our own ultimate benefit, the nectar of realisation, we
must have mastered the one taste of happiness and suffering.

Then after he attained enlightenment, the chiefs of humans and
gods, as far as the highest realms, showed him the greatest reverence,
placing his feet on the crown of their heads, and offering to serve
and honour him with all manner of delights. However, a Brahmin
called Bharadvaja abused him and criticized him a hundred times;
the impudent daughter of another Brahmin accused him of sexual
misconduct; he lived off rotten horse fodder for three months in
the land of King Agnidatta, and so on. But he remained without
the slightest fluctuation in his mind, neither elated nor downcast,
like Mount Meru unshaken by the wind. He showed that in order
to accomplish the benefit of sentient beings, again we need to have
mastered that equal taste of happiness and unhappiness.

So we practice this on ourselves, and with what happens to us. It is about our emotions, how we react, how our habitual tendencies are. That is what we need to work on. We need to work on this moment of our feeling, this moment of what's going on. That is the practice.

The result is not something for which you have to wait for many years, and after which it may or may not come. The result is now - how I am able to deal with what is going on right now. Whether, at this very moment, I can deal with whatever emotions, whatever strong reactions are going on. Happiness, loss of happiness, worries, sadness, fear, all sorts of things. If I can allow them to pass me by, if I can relax in that, if I can act or react in such a way that it is not a big problem, that I can deal with that, and I'm okay with that, then I possess the result of the practice in this moment.

So, what we need to do is use the training. Use it again and again and again. How much we practice is how much we use this on ourselves. It is not about how many months we go away into some strange place, shut up in a retreat, whatever you like to call it. It is not about how many prayers we do, how many mantras we recite, how many conferences we attend or how many degrees we get. The practice is not that. It is to integrate this understanding into ourselves. And, if we can do it for one moment, with just one problem, then that is the practice we have done.

So, if we can deal with just one small thing, one problem, one emotion, we have accomplished the practice that much, and we can get that much confidence for the next moment. So therefore you do it again and again and again. Whenever it is needed, you do just that. Use your understanding, use that experience, use that practice on yourself and when you know that this is something you can do, as the text says, whenever you need it, you have it, like a good friend. A good friend is someone who you can call whenever you need help, and they will come and help you. So in the same way, this teaching is like a good friend, or like a good doctor. In a way, you don't need anything else, you become self-sufficient, independent; able to stand on your own feet. And that is necessary; that is what we need to learn.

Working in that way is what we call practice. We don't need advice on everything. We say that we need teachers and gurus to teach us how to do this. But we don't need somebody to breathe down our necks all the time. We don't need somebody who is criticising us all the time, or complaining about us all the time, or controlling us all the time, that is not what we need. We need somebody to teach us how to do this, so that we can become independent, free, so that we know what practice is all about. We need discipline, we need patience and we need to do it for ourselves. It is not something that somebody else can do for me. Nobody else can do anything for me that will replace my own practice.

Of course, sometimes we pray and I think we can get blessings through that. Most probably we can get blessings – I am sure we can get blessings! But how much blessing I get does not depend on how much blessing somebody else is giving. How much blessing I get is how much blessing I am able *to receive*. From a Buddhist point of view, the Buddhas are trying to give blessing all the time, it is never the case that a Buddha withholds blessings. Otherwise he or she is not a Buddha.

So, how much blessing I receive does not depend on how much blessing a Buddha is giving me 'because he is pleased with me.' It depends on how much I can receive because I open myself to those blessings. If I practice, if I really work on opening my heart, then I receive blessing, whether the Buddhas like it or not; they cannot help themselves but to give blessing.

So, therefore, blessing is also not dependent on somebody else, it is dependent on me. This is how to understand it, this is the practice. How do we know whether we have practised or not? By knowing how free and independent we really feel; how much confidence we have that we can deal with our life, deal with whatever happens.

That is the practice. It's not that anger is finished and I have no more anger, that I have no more suffering, suffering is finished, I cannot ever be unhappy again. I cannot be angry at all. I can never be upset again. It does not happen like that. If it did, we would all end up like zombies!

I think even very highly realised beings can become happy, can become sad, can become upset, and can become ill sometimes. But they know how to deal with it, so that it is not a big deal. It is well known that His Holiness the Dalai Lama promotes a dialogue about meditation with Western scientists, and many important scientists have been observing him very closely. I'm not sure whether they have done brain scans or what - the details have not been disclosed - but they are making detailed studies of him. They say that they observe him expressing emotions very clearly: he can be sad, he can be upset, he can be angry. He expresses his emotions as much as, and in the same way as, anybody else. But he changes very quickly. He expresses his emotions, he feels them fully, but they don't stay. They change extremely fast.

To show this, from another source: somebody wrote once that they were in a discussion group with His Holiness, when sudden news arrived that a child in the Tibetan children's village school had died. They said they could see his emotions - his face completely changed and he was shedding tears, like a father who had lost his child. They could see that he was really sad; he didn't hide it. But a few moments later, he was okay again. He could laugh his heartiest laugh. That is something very special about him, that he can have a very intense feeling, but then have another, different one, very soon afterwards.

If we have learned how to deal with our emotions, and how to take life, it's not that we have no emotions, no thoughts, but that we have learned how to deal with them. We have learned how to work with those things and how to bear them so that they do not become a big problem, which overwhelms us.

And if you can do that, then you have learned how to liberate yourself. Sometimes this is called 'self-liberating thoughts and emotions.' Self-liberating something means you recognise it, and you know it so well that it cannot take root in your mind, you don't need to make an effort to eliminate it. By your understanding, by your confidence, by your practical knowledge, it just goes – because you let it go. And that is the most important thing. When that happens, then you can be stable, whatever situation you are in. Even the Buddha had to endure some very difficult situations, as the examples in the root text have shown.

Afterword

A teaching like this should really be taught by the Kadampa masters, whose very lives enacted their saying:

> *"No complaints when there is suffering,*
> *Great renunciation when there is happiness."*

But if someone like me explains it, then I'm sure that even my own tongue is going to get fed up and cringe with embarrassment. Still, with the sole aim of making one taste of all the worldly preoccupations, I, the old beggar Tenpé Nyima, coming from Shangnongkila (the forest of many birds) have written this, here.

Do Drupchen Rinpoche is showing his humility in saying this is not something that a person like himself, who is not so great, should be teaching. It should be something for the great masters of the Kadampa school, who have accomplished this kind of teaching. And he signed himself, 'old beggar Tenpe Nyima.'

Although the Third Do Drupchen was a very great master, he did not invent this teaching himself. It is based on the key Mahayana teaching called the Bodhicharyavatara, as well as many other teachings.

Question: Integrating practice

Student: Is it possible to integrate one's daily work and life into the path?

Rinpoche: That is supposed to be the practice and, actually, that is the only practice: integrating our daily life, including working or not working, or whatever you are doing, with the path. Using whatever instructions and understanding you have in your life, that is the practice. If you can do that, then practice is being done. If you cannot do it, then practice is not done. That is the whole point.

Student: If it is possible, can you tell us more about how to do that?

Rinpoche: I think this has been the subject of the entire teaching. As I have said again and again and mentioned earlier, it is not something that you can just be told how to do, and then do. It is something that we need to work at on our own, like learning how to ride a bicycle. It is something that can be taught, but at the same time cannot be taught. That is the problem.

Student: Is there a minimum of formal practice necessary or recommended as a reminder, in order to not lose the path or forget about the teachings, in order not to lose a good connection to the Dharma and its teachers?

Rinpoche: The main thing in order to not lose the connection with the Dharma is to understand, to remind yourself, what the practice is all about. It's not about doing pujas or doing rituals or things like that. It's about recollecting the teachings and the practice. That's the main thing. There is nothing called the minimum or the maximum in Buddhism, that I know of. It is about you: how quickly you want to transform. If I have no hurry, then I have no hurry; there is no minimum. If I am in a little bit of a hurry, then I am in a little bit of a hurry; then there is no maximum. So, it's up to you.

As much as you can, as much as you wish, as much as is possible, anything is good, better than nothing. But there is nothing like: "Oh, that's too much." Of course, you should do it in the proper way. If you make yourself go crazy, then it is too much.

Question: The wrong direction

Student: Would you warn us if you felt that we were going in the wrong direction? If you thought we might spoil our path and our opportunity to work on our karma in this life?

Rinpoche: I would warn someone, yes. But the problem is knowing when to warn them. That I don't know. I think if we read the teachings, or listen to some of the teachings, and then look at ourselves, where we are, who we are and what we are doing, then we will realise whether we are going in the right direction or the wrong direction. I don't think it is very easy for somebody else to tell you. Because it is not easy to see what is really going on. As I said, the practice is inside: how you are dealing with yourself, your own affairs, your own emotions, your own happiness. That is the practice; it is not outside. Therefore, it is difficult to say.

Shantideva, who wrote the *Bodhicharyavatara*, looked as if he was a really awful student when he was at Nalanda University. He did absolutely nothing, he just slept all day. He was called *Bu-su-ku* by the other students, because he seemed to be doing nothing: these are three root syllables which, in Sanskrit, mean eating, sleeping and defecating.

The university was so embarrassed by him and found him such a disgrace that they wanted to expel him, but they couldn't find any excuse to do this because he didn't break any rules, he didn't do anything wrong. So they found an indirect way to try to cause him to leave. They made a plan to ask everybody to give a teaching and they asked him to be the first. They thought that, since he clearly didn't know anything, because he didn't study, he would feel ashamed and run away. When they asked him to give a teaching, they set up a big throne and everybody came, but just to embarrass him. But he ascended the throne and gave an amazing, beautiful teaching. They were all shocked.

So you never know whether someone else is really practising or not. Shantideva didn't do any pujas, he didn't go to teachings, he didn't even perform any good works. That is how it was with him. But he was actually very accomplished. So therefore it is important to look at yourself.

Question: Motivation

Student: His Holiness the Dalai Lama often says that the most important thing is the motivation with which we do something. How much can a good motivation really compensate for a lack of skill, at least in certain aspects concerning one's own karma and the damage possibly done to others by unskillful actions?

Rinpoche: If you have a really good, positive motivation, then you will do your best to find out what is the best way to act for any given situation. Now, if you really try your best to find out what is the best thing to do and then act according to that, there is nothing better you can do. Because you cannot do anything better than trying your best, in terms of skillful means. Every one of us has some capacity to understand, to know. Mind has the capacity to know, the capacity to learn, the capacity for wisdom. If you really use it to your best ability, most probably you will do okay.

Yet sometimes we say, "I have acted with the best possible motivation," but when we look deeply, there is something that is not so clear in our motivation. And you may honestly act with a very good motivation and yet, most of the time, the result may not be the best. But this is okay, because we do the best that we can do, so therefore there is nothing else we could have done. There is no more we can do than our best. To have good motivation does not mean that we never make any mistakes, but we can do nothing better. So, therefore, that has to be enough, which is why our motivation becomes very, very important.

It can happen that we do something not so nice to others and then say we did it with good motivation. Sometimes we need to examine this motivation, because we think we acted with a good motivation, but there are some loopholes, some little things that we don't want to accept, or admit. This is why His Holiness always said that we need to examine our motivation again and again and really look into ourselves. This is important.

Question: Patience

Student: How can I develop more patience with myself if I can't see myself changing any habits for the better, even though I have been trying? Or maybe my question should be: how *not* to be patient, but finally change?!

Rinpoche: Well, to change oneself requires not only patience, but also allowing ourselves to change. We have lots of resistance to change. We all like what is familiar. We are all comfortable with what has been going on. Even if our situation is problematic, we don't like to go into unfamiliarity. We sometimes prefer to continue with what we are already experiencing, even if it is not pleasant, rather than move into something new, which we don't know about, which we are afraid of. So it is difficult to let go of habits and what is familiar. There is a story which illustrates this difficulty well:

Someone was in hell for countless years. Then, finally, after many centuries, their time was finished. When that person was coming out, he looked down and said, "Don't let anybody sit on my seat!" Someone would want to reserve his seat in hell?! Whether this really happened or not, it shows how difficult it is to allow ourselves to change. We could even have some attachment to hell: "This is *my* seat; I don't want anybody else to sit on it." It is like that. Therefore, we really need to learn to let go, that is the important thing. But changing is not easy. So we need to dare to let our habits go. Some daring is important. And commitment is important too.

———

Surmounting unhappiness, sorrow and pain as well as happiness and joy enables us to do something purposeful and to practise the Dharma. As long as we are in a state of sorrow, we cannot do anything beneficial, because we are overwhelmed by, and under the power of, our suffering and grief. Likewise, as long as we are in a state of joy, we also cannot do anything meaningful, because we have no time. Both states are useless.

It is crucial to work on these states because that will give us time - even if we are unhappy, we can have time; even if we are happy, we have time. Of course, we need to be practical: we have to care for ourselves and think about our future, but there is no purpose in exaggerating things. Training in acknowledging and appreciating sorrow and joy for what they are, opens the door to a useful and meaningful life.

Having trained, it does not matter where we live, as the text said: whether we are in solitude, whether in meditation in a retreat, whether at work in a busy town or city - all places are okay. Dharma practice is not restricted to a location, but means working on our mind, working on our emotions, working on happiness and unhappiness and dealing with suffering and grief. When we work on those facets of our lives, then we are practising Dharma. When we are not working on our mind, we are not practising Dharma, even if we recite mantras all day. If we really define the practice of Dharma, then we know that not working on the mind is not Dharma practice; even if we are convinced we are meditating, reciting mantras and engaging in good activities.

Practising the Dharma does not require a lot of time. It is not a question of time, but a question of discipline and working with our own mind, no matter who or where we are. Any place is good enough and any time is appropriate. Every moment of consciousness is the right time to practise the Dharma because we are working on our mind. Furthermore, society and relationships need not present any obstacle either, because we are working on ourselves. Even a gloomy environment offers a good opportunity to practise Dharma. Even a sophisticated society presents a good possibility to practise Dharma. Whatever happens to us is okay. If many good things happen, even if we are very prosperous and have a fortune, it is okay. If many negative things happen, even if we are poor and out of work, it is okay. If we are praised, popular and famous, it is okay. If nobody likes us, it is also okay. Even if we are criticised and mobbed, it is still okay.

If we can work within ourselves, practically and experientially, and come to know that sorrow and joy arise from our own way of reacting and do not depend upon what others say or do, or don't say or do, then we become a little bit fearless. Only then can the depth of our comprehension and our knowledge penetrate our being. This is the reason why it is often stated that at that time you become like a lion in the snow. We have the legend of the snow lion in Tibet: the snow lion just jumps over the snow and springs through the middle of avalanches, remaining untouched and unharmed all the while. I don't know whether snow lions actually exist or not - some people claim they do and others say they don't – but it gives an idea about how we need to be.

In this way, whatever we do, whatever happens, we are at ease within and have peace of mind: the most important thing. Nothing disturbs us anymore when we have peace of mind. We become truly happy and are able to lead a meaningful life. Maybe it then becomes possible to do things for others. In any case, we have done something for ourselves, by having found peace.

It is said that there is no real suffering for a Bodhisattva: he or she sees the way things are and doesn't suffer. They realise that there is no solid or fixed thing; that there are good times and hard times. They see that many things come together as they should, and many things come together as they should not; but everything passes.

Dedication

All my babbling,
In the name of Dharma
Has been set down faithfully
By my dear students of pure vision.

I pray that at least a fraction of the wisdom
Of those enlightened teachers
Who tirelessly trained me
Shines through this mass of incoherence.

May the sincere efforts of all those
Who have worked tirelessly
Result in spreading the true meaning of Dharma
To all who are inspired to know.

May this help dispel the darkness of ignorance
In the minds of all living beings
And lead them to complete realisation
Free from all fear.

Ringu Tulku

Glossary and Notes

Editor's Note: Wherever possible the descriptions in the glossaries of the Heart Wisdom books include Ringu Tulku's own words, gathered from a variety of teaching sources. But, as this is not always possible, the glossary is offered as a help to the reader and not a definitive authority.

Avalokiteshvara (Sanskrit) or Chenrezig (Tibetan) is the embodiment of the compassionate aspect of the mind of the Buddhas. In Tibet he is represented in male form as Chenrezig and is revered as their patron deity. The most common forms depicted are the four-armed and the 1000-armed Chenrezig. Avalokiteshvara is also represented as Kuan Yin in the Chinese tradition and as Kwannon in the Japanese, both in female form. The mantra of Avalokiteshvara, Om Mani Padme Hung, is one of the most powerful and universal of all mantras.

Bodhicharyavatara (Sanskrit) also known as *The Bodhisattvacharyavatara* is an 8th century Mahayana text, outlining the path of the Bodhisattva. It was composed by Shantideva, a great scholar, at the famous Nalanda Monastery in Northern India. It found wide acclaim almost immediately in India and rapidly spread. It was translated into Tibetan during the 9th century. It is the key text for anyone following the Bodhisattvayana (Mahayana) or Vajrayana path. There are many translations into English from several languages. One is *The Bodhisattva's Way of Life* translated by the Padmakara Translation Group from Tibetan, revised edition: Shambhala 2006.

Bodhicitta (*Bodhichitta* Sanskrit; *chang chub kyi sem* Tibetan) is the heart essence of the Buddha, of enlightenment. The root of the word, *Bodh*, means 'to know, to have the full understanding' and *citta* refers to the heart-mind or 'heart feeling.' In a practical sense, Bodhicitta is compassion: compassion imbued with wisdom.

Bodhisattva (Sanskrit; *changchub sempa* Tibetan) comes from the root *bodh* which means to know, to have the full understanding. The term describes a being that has made a commitment to work for the benefit of others to bring them to a state of lasting peace and happiness and freedom from all suffering. A Bodhisattva does not have to be a Buddhist but can come from any spiritual tradition or none. The key thing is that they have this compassionate wish to free all beings from suffering, informed by the wisdom of knowing this freedom is possible.

Buddhanature / Buddha nature (*Sugatagarba* Sanskrit; *desheg nyingpo* Tibetan) refers to the fundamental, true nature of all beings, free from all obscurations and distortions. Ultimately, our true nature, and the true nature of all beings, is inseparable from the nature of Buddha. It is the 'primordial goodness' of sentient beings, an innate all-pervasive primordial purity.

Chöd (Tibetan), literally meaning 'cutting through,' is a practice based on the Prajnaparamita Sutra (see below). The realised Tibetan female teacher, Machig Labdrön, set down the system of practice, after having received teachings from the Indian Mahasiddha Padampa Sangyé. The purpose of the practice is to cut through all aversion and attachment, all ego-clinging or clinging to a 'self.'

Dharma (Sanskrit; *chö* Tibetan) The word dharma has many uses. In its widest sense, it means all that can be known, or the way things are. The other main meaning is the teachings of the Buddha; also called the *Buddhadharma*.

Dzogchen (Tibetan; *Ati Yoga* Sanskrit) literally translates as 'Great Completion' or 'Great Perfection.' It is a body of teachings and practices that are considered to be the highest of the Inner Tantra of the Nyingma School of Tibetan Buddhism. They are aimed at helping a practitioner to recognize and abide in primordial true nature, the uncontrived, pure natural state. The practice of Dzogchen ultimately brings the same result as Mahamudra.

Emptiness (*shunyata* Sanskrit; *tong pa nyi* Tibetan) The Buddha taught in the second turning of the wheel of Dharma, that all phenomena have no real, independent existence of their own. They only appear to exist as separate, nameable entities because of the way we commonly, conceptually, see things. But in themselves, all things are 'empty' of inherent existence. This includes our 'self,' which we habitually unconsciously mistake to be an independently-existing, separate phenomenon. Instead, everything exists in an interdependent way and this is what the term emptiness refers to. As Ringu Tulku says in *Like Dreams and Clouds* Bodhicharya Publications: 2011: 'Emptiness does not mean there is nothing; emptiness means the way everything is, the way everything magically manifests.'

Four Powers are found in the practice of Vajrasattva. They are the powers of Reliance, Regret, Resolve and Remedy; and together form the basis for purification.

Karma (Sanskrit; *lay* Tibetan) literally means 'action.' It refers to the cycle of cause and effect that is set up through our actions. Actions coloured or motivated by *klesha* (see below), for example, anger or desire, will tend to create results in keeping with that action and also increase our tendency to do similar actions. These tendencies become ingrained in us and become our habitual way of being, which is our karma. According to our level of awareness, we can change our karma through consciously refining our actions.

Lama (Tibetan; *guru* Sanskrit) means teacher or master. *La* refers to there being nobody higher in terms of spiritual accomplishment and *ma* refers to compassion like a mother. Thus both wisdom and compassion are brought to fruition together in the lama. The word has the connotation of 'heavy' or 'weighty,' indicating the guru or lama is heavy with positive attributes and kindness.

Longchen Nyingthik are the main Nyingma teachings on Dzogchen, 'The Great Perfection.'

Mahayana (Sanskrit; *tek pa chen po* Tibetan) translates as 'Great Vehicle.' This is the second vehicle of Buddhism, and emphasises the teachings on Bodhicitta, compassion, and interdependence. It expands on the teachings of the Sravakayana (the foundational vehicle of Buddhism) and sees the purpose of enlightenment as being the liberation of *all* sentient beings from suffering, as well as oneself. This is the path of the Bodhisattva (see above) and so may also be called the Bodhisattvayana.

Nirvana (Sanskrit; *nyangde* Tibetan) literally means 'extinguished' and is the state of being free from all suffering. It is the opposite of samsara and arises when we have completely done away with all the obscurations, misunderstandings, negative emotions and other hindrances that create samsaric existence. When we are free from all fear and suffering and our mind is completely clear; this is described as enlightenment or nirvana.

Patrul Rinpoche (1808 - 1887) was an outstanding master of Tibetan Buddhism of the 19th century. He was a great scholar and Dzogchen master who wrote the *Words of My Perfect Teacher*, a classic for the Nyingma school. Some of the most important living Dzogchen and Mahamudra lineage teachings today, came from Patrul Rinpoche.

Refuge is about laying a foundation for practice, about finding a purpose and a path you wish to follow and making a clear decision or commitment to do that. In Buddhism, we take refuge in the 'Three Jewels:' Buddha, Dharma and Sangha. Buddha represents the example or possibility for us of complete transformation; Dharma provides the methods and trainings to develop towards that and Sangha is the community of practitioners who have some experience of this and so can inspire and support us on this path.

Renunciation is the firm wish to be free of the state of suffering that characterises the samsaric state of mind. This includes understanding we have the possibility for achieving freedom and having a willingness to dedicate one's life to achieving it. True renunciation happens within the heart and mind and does not include turning away from the world. In actuality, it increases our compassion and care for all other beings.

Rinpoche (Tibetan) is an honorific term in the Tibetan Buddhist tradition, reserved for great masters. It refers to how precious it is that such teachers are among us; literally translating as 'precious one.'

Samadhi (Sanskrit; *ting nge zin* Tibetan) A state of meditative absorption in which the mind rests unwaveringly.

Samsara / samsaric (Sanskrit; *khor wa* Tibetan) is the state of suffering of 'cyclical existence.' It describes a state of mind that experiences gross and / or subtle pain and dissatisfaction. It arises because the mind is deluded and unclear and thus perpetually conditioned by attachment, aversion and ignorance.

Shunyata *see Emptiness.*

Tantra (Sanskrit; *gyü* Tibetan) literally means 'continuity' or continuous thread (of the pure nature of mind) that runs through everything. In Buddhism, it also refers to the meditative practices of the Vajrayana, which include mantra recitation, visualisation practices, and the texts that describe these.

Tonglen (Tibetan) literally means 'sending and taking' and refers to the meditation associated with the Lojong (Mind Training) teachings of the Mahayana Vehicle of Buddhism. One visualises sending out love and happiness and healing light, while taking in the sufferings of the world, visualised as a thick black smoke. The visualisation rides the out and in breath in this way and works on our own mind and our view - our clinging to a self, separate from others, which must be protected over others. The reverse psychology of the meditation thus helps uproot our wrong assumptions, in a tangible and heart-felt way.

Editor's Note: Throughout the Heart Wisdom series we have used the word *student* to identify questions and discussion from audience members. This is not intended to imply the speaker would necessarily identify themselves as students of Tibetan Buddhism or of Ringu Tulku. It refers to the fact that they are being a 'student,' just in this instance, by virtue of asking a question in order to understand more.

Acknowledgements

With many thanks to David Cowey for initiating this project by providing the first draft of his edit of Ringu Tulku's teaching given at Bodhicharya Berlin in 2010. Assisted by transcription by Birgit Khoury and Tara Woolnough, his inspiration as a student took the shape of writing up this teaching of Rinpoche's to share it with others. I then took on the task of further editing and polishing of that text, and brought in some short but particularly inspiring passages from another occasion on which Rinpoche taught on this subject, which had been transcribed and partially edited by Gabriele Hollmann. Later, with editorial comments and input from Maeve O'Sullivan, a final edit brought this text through to completion, ready for publication. Thank you to all these editors and transcribers.

Proof-reading at various stages was provided by Mariette van Lieshout, for which we are very grateful, as well as for last proof reading comments provided by David Tuffield. We continue to value greatly Rachel Moffitt's organisation and administration of Bodhicharya Publications, which keeps everything together and oversees the printing and distribution of our books. Paul O'Connor provides all the layout and design aspects of our books. Thank you Paul for bringing the essence of these teachings out in this beautiful cover design and for the clear presentation of the words within.

The translation of the root text given in this text, is based on that of Adam Pearcey, 2006, with some very little additions from Ringu Tulku's own teaching as he went through. We would like to thank

Adam Pearcey very much for allowing the publication of his translation as part of this small book [Please refer to www.lotsawahouse.org for his full translation].

I would also like to thank the centres at which I stayed in order to work on this text. In our busy world, oases of calm and spaciousness are so important to free our minds enough that they can concentrate on teachings such as these presented here, so that they can really be heard and give us some chance to bring them into our lives (as well as editing and presenting them appropriately!). Thank you to Holy Isle in Scotland, Dzogchen Beara in Ireland and Tara Rokpa Centre in South Africa, for holding such spaces and welcoming guests to come and make good use of them.

Our final thanks goes, as always, to Ringu Tulku, for his patience in delivering these teachings so widely and inexhaustibly. It feels like he really listens to his students, to audience members and to people he meets everywhere, so that his teachings and answers to questions meet us where we are and address the problems people genuinely have. May we do this effort justice by putting these teachings here into practice. That is the real thanks we can give: to free ourselves, and others, from suffering wherever we can.

Mary Dechen Jinpa
On behalf of Bodhicharya Publications
Dzogchen Beara, Ireland, September 2018

About the Author

Ringu Tulku Rinpoche is a Tibetan Buddhist Master of the Kagyu Order. He was trained in all schools of Tibetan Buddhism under many great masters including HH the 16th Gyalwang Karmapa and HH Dilgo Khyentse Rinpoche. He took his formal education at Namgyal Institute of Tibetology, Sikkim and Sampurnananda Sanskrit University, Varanasi, India. He served as Tibetan Textbook Writer and Professor of Tibetan Studies in Sikkim for 25 years.

Since 1990, he has been travelling and teaching Buddhism and meditation in Europe, America, Canada, Australia and Asia. He participates in various interfaith and 'Science and Buddhism' dialogues and is the author of several books on Buddhist topics. These include *Path to Buddhahood, Daring Steps, The Ri-me Philosophy of Jamgon Kongtrul the Great, Confusion Arises as Wisdom*, the *Lazy Lama* series and the *Heart Wisdom* series, as well as several children's books, available in Tibetan and European languages.

He founded the organisations Bodhicharya - see www.bodhicharya.org and Rigul Trust - see www.rigultrust.org.

Other books by Ringu Tulku

Published by Bodhicharya Publications:

The Heart Wisdom Series:

- **The Ngöndro**
  Foundation Practices of Mahamudra
- **From Milk to Yoghurt**
  A Recipe for Living and Dying
- **Like Dreams and Clouds**
  Emptiness and Interdependence;
  Mahamudra and Dzogchen
- **Dealing with Emotions**
  Scattering the Clouds
- **Journey from Head to Heart**
  Along a Buddhist Path
- **Riding Stormy Waves**
  Victory over the Maras
- **Being Pure**
  The Practice of Vajrasattva
- **Radiance of the Heart**
  Kindness, Compassion, Bodhicitta
- **Meeting Challenges**
  Unshaken by Life's Ups and Downs

The Lazy Lama Series:

- **Buddhist Meditation**
- **The Four Noble Truths**
- **Refuge**
  Finding a Purpose and a Path
- **Bodhichitta**
  Awakening Compassion and Wisdom
- **Living without Fear and Anger**
- **Relaxing in Natural Awareness**
- **Loving Kindness**
  Our True Brave Heart

Other Titles:

- **Parables from the Heart**
  Teachings in the Tibetan Oral Tradition

Published by Shambhala:

- **Path to Buddhahood**
  Teachings on Gampopa's 'Jewel Ornament
  of Liberation'
- **Daring Steps**
  Traversing the Path of the Buddha
- **Mind Training**
- **The Ri-Me Philosophy of**
  Jamgon Kongtrul the Great
  A Study of the Buddhist Lineages of Tibet.
- **Confusion Arises as Wisdom**
  Gampopa's Heart Advice on the
  Path of Mahamudra.

Also available from Rigul Trust:

- **Chenrezig**
  The Practice of Compassion - A Commentary
- **The Boy who had a Dream**
  An illustrated book for children

For an up to date list of books by Ringu Tulku, please see the Books section at

www.bodhicharya.org

Our professional skills are given free of charge in order to produce these books, and Bodhicharya Publications is run by volunteers; so your purchase of this book goes entirely to fund further books and contribute to humanitarian and educational projects supported by Bodhicharya.

Thank you.

The Ringu Tulku Archive

THE RECORDED TEACHINGS OF RINGU TULKU RINPOCHE

www.bodhicharya.org/teachings